WIDE SKIES

FINDING A HOME IN THE WEST

Gary Holthaus

THE UNIVERSITY OF ARIZONA PRESS   TUCSON

The University of Arizona Press
Copyright © 1997
The Arizona Board of Regents
All rights reserved

♾ This book is printed on acid-free, archival-quality paper.
Manufactured in the United States of America

02 01 00 99 98 97   6 5 4 3 2 1

Library of Congress Cataloging-in-Publication Data

Holthaus, Gary H., 1932–
    Wide skies : finding a home in the West / Gary H. Holthaus.
        p.   cm.
    ISBN 0-8165-1672-3 (cloth : alk. paper).—
    ISBN 0-8165-1673-1 (pbk. : alk. paper)
    1. West (U.S.)—Description and travel.   2. Holthaus, Gary H.,
1932– —Journeys—West (U.S.)   3. Holthaus, Gary H., 1932– —
Homes and haunts—West (U.S.)   I. Title.
    F595.3H65—1997   97-4568
    917.804'33—dc21   CIP

British Library Cataloguing-in-Publication Data
A catalogue record for this book is available from the British Library.

Parts of this book are reproduced by courtesy of the publisher: "Coho
Smith" appeared in the *Alaska Quarterly Review* 16 (Fall/Winter 1997);
"The Dryland Farmer" appeared in a different version in *Halcyon* 14
(1992): 267–77; "Homeland" appeared in a different form as "Nature
Deserves 'A respect Agreeable'" in *Environ* 15 (Spring 1994): 20–25, and
as "Homeland" it is in *Northern Lights* 12, no. 2 (Winter 1996): 13–16;
"Rivers" appeared in *Arrested Rivers* (Niwot, Colo.: University Press of
Colorado, 1993), 52–66; "Sheep-Dip" was published in *Northern Lights* 9
(Winter 1994): 29; "Whiteout" was published in the *Alaska Quarterly
Review* 12 (Spring-Summer 1994): 33–38.

For my brother Jack and my friend Ben

When we say, "How well I remember!" we invariably remember poorly. It is the emotion that is strong, not the details.

—Wright Morris

Men's memories are uncertain and the past that was differs little from the past that was not.

—Cormac McCarthy

CONTENTS

Preface	xi
Acknowledgments	xvii
Homeland	3
Rivers	21
Signs of Hope	31
Falling behind the Data Curve	49
Descartes on the Kuskokwim	57
A Gentile Pilgrim in the Promised Land	59
A Little Western Advice	79
Gulls on a High Wind	81
Coho Smith	97
The Dryland Farmer	109
Sheep-Dip	119
Deer	127
Whiteout	133
At the Mercy of Warmth	141
At the Heart of the Heart of the Universe	157

PREFACE

East of Evanston, Wyoming, the sky is still dark and lightning strikes all along the horizon in the east and south. The sky flares and flickers like an old war movie. A coyote darts into the headlights' bright glare, wisely turns abruptly, and scoots back to the safety of the shadows. An Iowa boy who had lived for four years in Boston, a few years in Montana, and a quarter of a century in Alaska, I feel right at home in this dark continental vastness. Like many other Americans, judging from the amount of predawn traffic, I am on the move, scurrying through the dark like a coyote, nose down in pursuit of something—my work, an ephemeral desire that has no name, a life, an end to restlessness, a true place in the world.

You know this West; everyone in America knows it. You may recognize the trip, too. Perhaps you've made it yourself. We recognize the West, and the trip, for we have seen them in movies or photographs even if we have never strayed farther from home than the Bijou or the Strand or looked beyond the calendar on the wall. Some may think that northern New Mexico looks like Wyoming because the movie we saw called *Taos* was filmed in the headwaters of the Shoshone outside Cody. In the long run, it may not matter. The phrase "out West" conjures images in all our minds. Whether they are accurate may be less important than the connection they make to something vast.

We have read about this West, too, in books ranging from pulp novels to the works of Wallace Stegner, though our reading sometimes leaves us confused about what is real and what is myth. There have always been those who wanted to tell Wild West tales for profit or fame, and there have always been some who wanted to get the story straight, describing their personal experience as plainly as they could tell it in letters, diaries, fiction, poems, and essays. For every pulp writer like Ned Buntline there has been a cowboy like Andy Adams. Our storytellers of book or film have enshrined the West deep in our national consciousness, and whether mythical or real, pictures and stories of the West have shaped our vision of ourselves as Americans.

Our contemporary West is as conflicted as it ever was in its "wild" days. Some conflicts are within those people who see themselves as self-reliant but who depend on the federal government for subsidies in various forms, some more obvious than others. Other conflicts are social: love of the land and the necessity for employment generate painful conflicts between the employees of extractive industries and the environmentalists. Our rhetoric about freedom is contradicted by our oppression of minority workers who bend to do our harvesting and without whom much of our agriculture would fail. The care some environmentalists exhibit toward the land is negated by the indifference they show toward its human inhabitants and by their insistence that humans are part of nature yet have no place in the wilderness. Now laptop entrepreneurs who can afford it are moving in, and those who can't afford to stay, even after having lived in the region for generations, are moving out.

Living and traveling in the West, I found that the worries that plague westerners express themselves on three levels: one is defined by the media, the environment, and a particular history;

a second is found on the level of social or community life; the third is revealed in those underlying, fundamental human issues that we share with all others. These are not quite parallel, for the land, history, and society all have their effect on fundamental human questions, our responses to those questions affect the way we act in our social life, and our social life in turn affects the ways in which we cope with the never very deeply buried questions that arise from our personal tragedies and triumphs.

The media report western issues in terms of economic or environmental policy: water, public land, grazing, resource exploitation, "wise use," and individual rights versus state regulation. These concerns are real enough, and many westerners spend a great deal of time not just worrying about them but working on them. The issues arise from a unique landscape and a unique history; they are distinctly western. They are also dramatic and large-scale, pitting determined adversaries against one another as though on a dusty street at high noon and thus fit the western myth promoted by the old Hollywood movies. We think of these as "public issues."

But the West I know reveals itself in encounters on a small scale—the ordinary, the often overlooked. For years, while I have been developing public programs in the humanities, trying to bring historians, philosophers, archaeologists, linguists and their academic kin together with local folks, I have listened to people talk about themselves and their communities. The voices in the stories that follow are not generally those of policy analysts or pundits or government officials. They are the voices of people, mostly people in small towns, who are struggling to create a life for themselves and their neighbors. Their definition of the issues is not always that of the popular media, legislators, or the shapers of policy. The depth of these citizens' concerns, and their willingness to work at community building, are signs of hope not only for the West but for all of American democracy. Fretting about the economy is a given; everybody does it. Though environmental questions figure in the concerns of ordinary people working to create or re-create their communities, they are not necessarily foremost. When visiting small towns around the West and talking with people about the matters they find most disturbing, other issues come to the surface with compelling force: education, a general withdrawal from public life, and an increasingly overt racism.

But there is also a deeper, often unspoken, level of concern. Ranchers, business people, teachers, miners, loggers, doctors, and college professors all consider fundamental philosophical questions that are profoundly human and therefore universal. Why do the innocent suffer? Who am I, and why have I been given this life? What is the nature of the universe? These are the concerns of persons in every age and in every place, whether continent or tiny island. If these matters are indeed universal, they must be ordinary too. We refer to these issues as personal or private issues, yet they are the most widely shared of all. Nevertheless, they rarely rise to any public level and are not featured in the daily newspaper or the evening news, although they may be what TV reporters are trying—and failing—to get at when they ask people at the scene of a tragedy or the celebration of a championship victory, How do you feel right now?

After bumping around the West afoot or horseback—or most often hastening the fossil fuel burnout in an automobile—I can report that there is no part of the West that is at ease. It is a regional teapot in which all the world's tempestuous conflicts, contradictions, and questions simmer and boil. In the stories that follow, you will meet some pretty fine people, accomplished and intelligent, who wrestle with issues at each of these levels—struggling, it often seems, with "principalities and powers."

Where is the West? My own sense of the West includes the prairies that rise from the central Dakotas through central Nebraska, Kansas, Oklahoma, and Texas, and it flows over the Rockies and across the high deserts of the Colorado Plateau and eastern Oregon and Washington, a line that extends roughly from Yakima through Baker and Reno. I haven't included the West Coast here because the ecology west of the Sierras and the Cascades shifts so dramatically and the population swells to numbers that most "westerners" couldn't abide. As a friend once said, "I grew up in L.A. and had to drive twelve hundred miles east to get out West. But I could tell this is a different world, and I'm glad I made the trip!" My notion of the West also includes Alaska, which may come as a surprise to some who do not know that state well.

Alaska has more in common with this region than it does with the Northwest Coast, with which it is often linked, and like many Alaskans I have come to include it in the West. Like Montana, Wyoming, Arizona, New Mexico, and most other western states, Alaska has large federal landholdings, extensive areas of Indian land, and a diverse population thinly dispersed across a huge and equally diverse geography. Urban areas in western states are often small by the standards of other states and frequently are concentrated in just two major towns: Anchorage and Fairbanks; Billings and Great Falls; Cheyenne and Casper; Phoenix and Tucson; Denver and Colorado Springs; Albuquerque and Santa Fe. All of the states have a history of resource exploitation, and their legislators still vote to protect extractive industries. Though it varies from time to time and place to place, there is a common anti-intellectual attitude among many citizens, a contradictory appreciation of reading, and an atmosphere in which legislatures have a hard time supporting education at any level. In all these states the weather can be severe and the land harsh and extraordinarily beautiful.

The West has been home to many cultures, but for most modern Americans, home is a hard place to identify. Most of us grew up someplace other than our current residence. Americans have always been on the move, especially since World War II, and our extended families no longer provide a sense of place or of home. Most of us struggle to create a home in a new region. I, like many other Americans, am among the world's most restless and uprooted peoples; questions about home arise daily.

The question of home, the public issues we wrestle with in our local communities, what some philosophers call "the problem of evil" or "the problem of suffering"—all these matters have moved me over a lifetime, and the West and westerners have taught me something about them.

In telling these stories about traveling the West, visiting with people who worry about their communities or about how to hold on to the home place that has been in the family for generations or centuries, I have been pushed to reconsider my own history, my sense of what a homeland might mean, to think again about what it means to find our way in the world and be at home in it.

These stories, then, come from traveling again in the places I've lived and places new to me. I have tried to recreate in these pages the West of my own memory and consciousness as well as the real West I encountered along the way. This is a journey that touches the land and the lives of many throughout the arid West and Alaska. It inevitably becomes a personal odyssey as well, a story of finding my way and losing it, of coming to grips with loss, and learning, as Mary Oliver so perfectly put it, "to love this world," hoping to balance the harm one does with something of value, and discovering those signs of hope that we all must nourish. Finally, this is a journey always headed toward home, the story of a life lived in the region and experiences that connect the current West to the Hollywood West of the grade B movies I grew up on.

ACKNOWLEDGMENTS

As with any book, this one owes thanks to a host of friends. It would never have been undertaken if Rick Vollertsen, an old Alaska friend, had not challenged, threatened, and cajoled me. Ted Chamberlin, Professor of Comparative Literature at the University of Toronto, read it all and offered encouragement as well as suggestions. Steven Epstein, Professor of History at the University of Colorado and perhaps the most widely read historian I have ever known, also read it all and offered his support in myriad ways. I used to have children; now I have adults: Kevin and Stephanie, son and daughter. Both read it and still said, "Do it."

Additional thanks go to Dorik Mechau and Carolyn Servid, old friends in many adventures; and to John Stevenson, Chuck Squire, Reg Saner, Katheryn Rios, Jeffrey Robinson, Linda Hogan, Brad Johnson, Tom Lyon, Jim McVey, and many others in the English Department at the University of Colorado. One couldn't ask for finer companions along the way. The eloquent oil paintings of Chuck Forsman, also of the University of Colorado, triggered the chapter called "Rivers," and Charles Wilkinson of the University of Colorado law school urged me to publish others. Some of the chapters began as papers for my classes in western American literature at the University of Colorado. My thanks go to all the students who proved such friends there.

Elliott West, Professor of History at the University of Arkansas, taught me much about the territory, and pressed me to think harder about it, during summer institutes for teachers sponsored by the National Endowment for the Humanities. My Social Science Education Consortium colleagues Jim Giese, Barbara Miller, and Laurie Eastman all provided opportunities to sharpen ideas during those sessions, while Sylvia Thomas provided expert attention to the logistics and comfort of everyone.

Alvin Josephy, Jr., and Robert Utley have not only taught me much but have also inspired me with both their books and their lives. And thanks to Ron Spatz for his early faith. Carol Wilson and David Chrislip have supported all my efforts with their compassionate strength. Robert Hedin, with his fine poet's eye, offered an especially helpful critique of some portions of the text. So did David Foster, Distinguished Professor of Linguistics and Foreign Languages at Arizona State University. Luis Alberto Urrea also read and commented helpfully on some of these stories and has been a source of inspiration. Gary Snyder was the first to prompt me to write about my Alaskan experiences, and he, Gary Nabhan, Louise Erdrich, and writer/photographer Robert Adams all encouraged me to publish various parts of this book at various times. Thanks to Bill Kittredge, whose view of the West is critical for us all. My colleagues in things western—all directors of state humanities councils—Margaret Kingsland, Robert Young, Delmont Oswald, Judith Winseler, Tom McClanahan, Hidde Van Duym, Dick Lewis, and Jim Pierce gave me opportunities to find some of these stories and have always been a source of inspiration for me and of hope for the West. All provided marvelous hospitality and friendship before, during, and since my travels in their states. My thanks to them and to their humanities councils.

My thanks, too, to the National Endowment for the Humanities and to my colleagues there and in its state programs, and to the National Federation of State Humanities Councils. Both agencies not only tolerated but supported my peregrinations and much else besides. After twenty-five years of close association, I remain a true believer in both organizations and in the humanities as well. And always, to Lauren Pelon, who makes everything beautiful.

WIDE SKIES

HOMELAND

On summer afternoons huge cumulus clouds drifted over Montana's Hellroaring Plateau, and feisty nimbus dumped cold rain in squalls so small that the sun remained out as they rolled through the wide skies. Fishermen got soaked and sunburned at the same time. Paradise for me was a hike across the alpine tundra and rocks to Sliderock Lake or around a gravelly point and down the scree into Moon Lake. Moon, above timberline, was home to cutthroat trout, and the rocks along the shore were home to coneys and marmots.

The first time I was up there was on a July afternoon in 1958. I was with Jim Croft and Bob DeVries. Bob was a rancher and dryland farmer from Roberts, and Jim ran the grain elevator there. Both liked to visit Sliderock Lake and fish for brook trout whose flesh was pink from feasting on the freshwater shrimp that swarmed in the dark lake. We rode Jim's old pickup, bouncing up the gravel too fast because it was already late.

We parked on top and walked over to Sliderock. I thought those guys were running. I'd been in Iowa and Boston, at sea level or not much above it, for twenty-six years. Montana's 10,000-foot elevation left me gasping and lurching to keep up. For a while they "flailed the water" with their fly lines, as Bob put it, while I tried to remember what Pete McCall, my first fly-fishing mentor, had taught me down in Colorado years before. Nobody caught anything, and we soon strolled, at what seemed to me breakneck speed, back to the pickup.

On the way down, sitting at the righthand window, I could see what I had missed on the way up: precipitous slopes sheering off my side of the truck and falling over jumbled rock and the occasional dwarfed spruce to the canyon bottom hundreds of feet below. I stared with what I hoped passed for aplomb as the pickup lurched and swayed, hardly slowing for the switchbacks, flying headlong down into the light of its own headlights after the dark came suddenly.

The limit for a fisherman in those days was ten pounds plus one fish. That doesn't sound like much of a load, but when you are at the short end of a windy afternoon, dehydrated from the sun, wet from a squall, and staring up at the scree and trying to figure out the best way to climb, the extra weight can seem like a real burden. If you are climbing right up the bare rock face, as Joe Reese, a professional fisherman and marine taxidermist from Florida, and I did once on our first time in to Moon Lake, that swinging canvas creel can seem not only heavy but dangerous. We found ourselves scrambling up, reaching as far above our heads as possible, laying the rod case down, hauling ourselves up to it, and reaching up again. When I looked down, there was nothing below but water, a visual trick of such country, where rocks will stop your body long before you hit water, despite appearances. When we got to the top, legs trembling, lungs rasping, we lay on our backs sucking in the thin air, glad to have done that, once, and vowing never to do it again. It would be almost ten days before we could make time to go back.

That first trip up into the Beartooth high country in Bob DeVries's pickup was like a trip home after a long time away. I could not know it for sure then, but somehow I felt it, understood that this country was in my bones already and would remain so. The connection was fragile because I was a tenderfoot, but I could learn, I thought. Maybe I'd never know the country as well as the men I hung out with, but I could develop in my own way, and I knew that, wherever I went, that country and those people would always be part of me.

When I was a boy in Iowa, the men in my family—my father and his cousins, my grandfather and his brother—were good horsemen and hunters and fishermen, and their word was their bond. They prided themselves on their knowledge of the fields and streams and their ability to fix things when they broke even when they could find no parts. They kept good guns—shotguns—and kept them cleaned and oiled. Shooting straight and fast was a cherished skill. They hunted pheasants and ducks, squirrels and cottontails in the cover of their Iowa farmland and dreamed of hunting deer and elk with rifles in the high Rockies. They fished for walleyes and northerns, bass and crappies and bluegills, using spoons and plugs in the murky streams and lakes of the Midwest, and they dreamed of fishing for trout with dry flies in fast mountain streams that ran clear most of the summer.

My uncle T.A. lived in Colorado and did fish for trout and hunt for deer. For my fourth birthday he sent me a big hat and a red neckerchief. Another time he sent chaps, and yet another a silver-trimmed belt with two holsters and two silver guns with ivory handles. The guns, the silver, and the ivory were not real, of course, but that fancy gear was a kind I thought all cowboys wore. After all, T.A. lived where cowboys lived. I admired Pop and T.A. and all those men and came to cherish the same dreams.

How could such cowboy values flourish in the thoroughly domesticated Midwest? When Pop was a boy, Iowa still had virgin timber on its eastern hills, the prairie beyond Omaha marked the beginning of the West, and the adjective most often associated with the West was *Wild*. People still knew and appreciated good horses, and most still depended on them for their field work and their transportation. Cars and tractors were just coming into the country when Pop came into his young manhood, but few could afford them. Everyone supplemented the garden produce, the slaughter hogs, and the chickens and eggs with rabbits, squirrels, pheasants, ducks, and fish. Being a good hand with a gun was still a useful talent and was therefore admired.

Pop's virtues, I realize now, were the pragmatic ones prized by nineteenth-century Europeans like my immigrant grandfather and by people throughout the western frontier. They were still valued in my father's youth by rural midwestern families who were on the edge of something new but didn't have much in the way of cash income. The reason Pop had frontier values when I was a child was that he had grown up a frontier child and farming country had not changed enough between his birth and my own to warrant a change in those values.

We tend to forget how recent the western past is, even this late in the game, as the future presses upon us so worrisomely. My father's life span—even my own—serves as a reminder: Pop was born just thirty years after George Armstrong Custer was killed, and just sixteen after Custer's remnant Seventh Cavalry devastated the Sioux at Wounded Knee. He could have known survivors of both those sad events. When Pop was born, Colonel Henry B. Carrington, the commander at Fort Phil Kearney when his arrogant young Captain William Fetterman was decoyed beyond help and killed by Red Cloud's warriors, was still writing books, and Red Cloud was still alive. Pop was born a year before Al Sieber, the legendary Arizona scout and nemesis of Geronimo, was crushed by a boulder, and Geronimo was still alive. Pop was already eleven when Buffalo Bill Cody died, thirteen when Teddy Roosevelt crossed the great divide, and twenty when Yellowstone Kelly, the famous Montana scout and guide for the first military expeditions into Yellowstone Park, published his autobiography. Pop's twentieth year was also the one in which Nelson A. Miles, Custer's contemporary and colleague, and a much meaner spirited and more ambitious man, went to his reward. Wyatt Earp was still refereeing boxing matches in California when Pop reached his majority, and Libby Custer, George's widow, was still alive when I was born. In that light the mythic West of the grade B movies of my childhood seems very recent.

Thanks to Pop and T.A., an interest in things western, especially horses, was early passed on to me. My first pony was blind, or nearly so. He'd spent most of his life underground at the bottom of a coal mine. The mine operators brought him up when they thought he might die after twenty years of pulling iron-wheeled carts full of coal through the dark mine to the elevator. He was black and white and little bigger than a Shetland pony, and he cost Pop ten dollars he had dredged up from the depths of the Depression. I was five or six, and that exhausted and rickety pony marked the beginning of dreams. His name was Pete, and after a few weeks on Grandpa's farm outside Greeley, Iowa, he looked fat and sleek, though other farm kids teased me about his rupture. His penis hung down like a piece of fire hose. I did not care; I rode him as if he were one of those beautiful horses of astonishing stamina that I watched on Saturday afternoons at the Strand. No cinematic car chase will ever seem as exciting as those hot pursuits on horses ridden by Johnny Mack Brown, Wild Bill Elliot, or the Black Whip. Even the villains rode animals so immaculately groomed, so lovely in their lines, that it was wondrous to see them running tirelessly past the same rock, the same leafless tree, one limb hanging out over the trail as if grown there especially for a hanging.

When I was twelve I got to spend a whole summer in Denver, living with Aunt Melba and Uncle T.A. Just a block beyond their house I hung little nooses, trying to catch the prairie dogs that, along with the sagebrush, were the only things visible between their house and the mountains. Late in the summer Uncle T.A. took Sam Hill, a retired school superintendent, and me off into the mountains because T.A. wanted to scout for deer. On the way the men talked of bears. When we parked on a high ridge that looked out over a considerable chunk of terrain, T.A.

suggested that we split up:"You go down that ridge and make a swing through the bottom. I'll go over on that other ridge, and Sam'll cover this pocket behind us."We were looking over a big country, and his plan seemed a bit scary to my twelve-year-old eye, given the previous conversation. I couldn't stop myself from asking in as adult a tone as I could muster, as if it were really a matter of no consequence but I just thought I'd check:"What do I do if I meet a bear?"T.A., straight-faced, said,"Spit in his eye." Sam smiled and said,"Most of us don't spit too good over our shoulder."

Such events, and the family stories they spawned, prepared me to be at home elsewhere than Iowa.The fact that Iowa came to feel less like home wasn't because I didn't know the place. I loved fall days in Iowa, hunting squirrels and pheasants, and the rich autumn light in the leaves of the oaks and maples. I knew the names of the trees and smaller plants and the habits of many local wild animals and birds. The idea of Iowa as home should have been embedded in me forever. Instead, as I drove the trac- tor on my uncle Bernard's farm near Calamus, picking up bales of sweet alfalfa, I thought about riding an Arizona bronc named Rabbit at my grandfather's old place in Greeley, and "real" hunt- ing and fishing were never far from my imagination. Bullheads were plentiful in the Wapsi (short for Wapsipinicon) on the cou- ple of rainy days when we got to go fishing, but they were not, I just knew, as satisfying as trout would be in the Rockies.

The first day I drove into Montana I felt as if I were arriving home. It was 1958 and at age twenty-six I was just beginning to find my place. I'd worked my way through college packing wheat in hundred-pound sacks for Quaker Oats and moving steel beams at Iowa Steel and Manufacturing. I'd completed three years of seminary at Boston University and had completed a master's program in historical theology during a fourth year while working in a retail store and serving as an assistant to the pastor of a large church in Reading, Massachusetts. Now I was headed west to work in three little churches in south central Montana just sixty miles from Billings and a few miles north of the Wyoming border. Red Lodge, Roberts, and Luther were nestled at the bottom of the Beartooth Mountains sixty-seven miles from the northeast corner of Yellowstone National Park. I'd never been there, but I knew this could be the place where I might realize all the boyhood dreams triggered by the desires and values the men in my family had shared through their stories.

It was drizzling, a typical June rain essential to the growth of alfalfa, to the irrigation that would be necessary throughout the summer, and in the high country to the snowpack that determined the amount of water that would be available in the future. All the way across eastern Montana to Billings we were in fabled landscape: home ground for the cattle kingdom, Lewis and Clark country, Hugh Glass country, Jim Bridger country. Finally we cut the Yellowstone near where John Colter set out to trade with the Crows. I knew Colter. Well, I didn't exactly *know* him, of course, but I knew he ran barefoot from the Blackfeet up near the Three Forks and that he looked like Clark Gable. I'd seen that in a movie, so scant on historical fact, so full of action, everything so . . . so black and white. I knew Hugh Glass, too, from reading *Lord Grizzly,* a book I'd picked up in Boston thinking I'd found another western only to discover that I'd found western literature.

It seemed as if I already knew the road, how the next turn would go, how the great ocean of the prairie would roll us in one direction or another. In my mind I could see the buffalo that had once cruised up and down what A. B. Guthrie called "these thousand hills" like endless pods of shaggy whales riding the prairie seas. I'd read Teddy Roosevelt and thought I could tell where he had once escorted, at great peril, a couple of hardcases back to town to be jailed.

This was home to trappers and branding irons and pine ridges and the Northern Cheyenne and legendary Miles City saddle makers who were geniuses with leather. L. A. Huffman was at home here, and his photos, despite the limited visibility permitted by the rain, were all around me. To my eye, nothing much had changed in this western landscape, and I was glad. It was home to elk and deer bounding toward one from the cover of *Outdoor Life* and of bears rearing up in one's face, and of great trout that could be caught on tiny flies if one only knew the right technique.

There was a kind of freedom in the drizzly air, guaranteed by open land where one could wander with danger present and disaster or death possible at every instant. There was also the freedom guaranteed by folks who never asked too closely where you hailed from or what you did, a notion I suppose I'd learned from reading about Buck Duane, the hero in Zane Gray's *Lone Star Ranger*. The past was not a danger here. The possibility of creating oneself anew was more real than anywhere else I'd ever been. That opportunity was in the air all around me, whether self-created or Hollywood inspired, falling like mist onto the arid land. It was as if I knew the territory even though I'd never been in it before, and I knew the stories and understood the mores, and they were all heroic or stoic, and the stoics were my heroes—how could one not feel inspired? In short, I was home.

In Red Lodge, Roberts, and Luther, while making the rounds and getting acquainted with church members, I was privileged to meet ranchers who, until the early fifties, pretty much did things the old way. That is, the cattlemen among them would get up in the morning, do chores, top off a horse apt to be cantankerous, and ride out to look over cows, check salt and water, and return. Unlike my movie heroes, they walked their horses every foot of the way unless, in short bursts, they had to catch a cow for a closer look. In winter they would feed their stock using a team and wagon, breaking open unwieldy bales for the cattle that, knowing the routine, would string out behind. It was not until 1948 that the Rural Electrification Administration had come to some of those ranches, and still later to the ranches in more remote areas. Even then a couple of the older men, bachelor brothers tucked away up a coulee just west of Red Lodge, continued to use kerosene out of habit or orneriness. The light from the windows in their ranch house glowed yellow in the evening. Surplus Jeeps were just coming into wide use, and most of the work was still done on horseback. As far as work was concerned, nothing much had changed since the 1890s.

I say "ranchers, . . . the cattlemen among them," because downcountry from Red Lodge and Luther the land turned dry and the ranching turned with it, to winter wheat and barley and dryland farming. The hills rolled away from the foot of the Beartooths to the long-ranging prairie that would flatten out, wavering in the heat shimmers, to the north, where wheat strips and summer fallow alternated on the horizon, stretching clear up into Alberta. To the east lay the Pryor Mountains—home to Plenty-Coups, the great Crow leader—and south of the Pryors the Bighorns rose where Red Cloud and Carrington, General Crook and Sitting Bull all worked out their destinies.

Between the east bench above Red Lodge and those blue-looming mountains lay some serious desert and badlands, drifting out from under the bench past the old coal mines at Bearcreek and beyond the arable land along the Clarks Fork to the Cottonwood country, where one could still see ancient pictographs known to few except Vern Waples, the game warden, who showed them to me. Vern had been working that country as a warden for thirty years and knew where the Crows had wintered along Sage Creek, and who had owned the deserted homesteads on Bowler Flat at the base of the Pryors, and where to find the wild horses that pastured on the high slopes in the summer, and where the ice caves at the top of the range led. No one I know will ever again travel that country on foot or horseback, in jeep or pickup truck the way Vern did, and no one will ever again know it as well.

From the top of the Pryors, along the rim where in earlier

days the Crows had laid out their dead, one looks over the Dry-head country and Bighorn Canyon, once the third largest canyon in the United States and not yet dammed and filled when I first stared down from its precipitous edge. Indians used to camp there in the bottoms, the women digging roots while the men chipped flints for hunting and war. I once walked up the canyon bottom with Vern, before the dam was built, feeling the presence of the deep past in the high rock walls and the ghosts from older times, finding mounds of flint shards and campsites scattered in the sage and yucca. Now the Bighorn is flooded, its full depth and range obscured, the old sites familiar to American Indians for thousands of years inundated, the old warriors' flint chips washed away by the rush of water sweeping in to fill the great gorge.

South, rising behind Red Lodge, lay the Beartooth Mountains, Mount Maurice to the east of the Rock Creek valley, and to the west Silver Run Plateau and Granite Peak, the highest point in the state. Up Rock Creek the valley broadened a bit and there were Forest Service campgrounds and, on the west side of the creek, a narrow gravel road that twisted along precipitous rock slides to the top of the Hellroaring Plateau. Folks called it the Chrome Road because it led to some abandoned chromium mines from which, during World War II, trucks laden with ore made their way down to the railhead. The remnants of that road were the path to the Hellroaring Plateau that Bob, Jim, and I took that first summer.

Montana isn't exactly the place where the West began for me. It began in those stories my dad and Uncle T.A. told, and in the books I'd read and the ponies I'd ridden. But Montana was the place where I first began to develop some personal experience of it and to make some personal investment in it, trying to understand the place, its history and literature, and the people who lived there. All this had something to do not only with the land but also with the people I came to know, the men and women whom I admired and who exhibited such patience with my greenhorn striving. They made a place for me, allowed me a space in their lives and their reality, let me ride along to check the cattle or bring them down from summer range to the home place or hunt jackrabbits on cold nights in February, and I felt honored.

Some folks find a home; others make their home. Mine came as a gift, given me by folks in Montana. Robert Frost was wrong. Home is not where, when you go there, they have to take you in. Home is where, when you go there, they take you in whether they have to or not.

My calling the West home may seem inappropriate to those who are third- or fourth-generation westerners, especially to those who fear the influx of California computer commuters, the fax folks and modem movers who are now flooding into the West in increasing numbers. It also raises questions about where home is for Americans today, for street people are not the only homeless people we have on our hands. Restless, moving, we Americans may be more homeless than any other culture the earth has ever seen, certainly far more homeless than the nomadic peoples of the nineteenth century and before. They knew the territory they wandered through, knew it in intimate detail. We do not take time to smell the flowers and wouldn't know their names if we did, yet nomadic Arab desert dwellers, American Indians, and wandering aboriginal Australians had a name for every plant and knew their uses as well. Who, then, is at home?

My insistence that Montana is home for me also raises a question about who is a westerner. We may believe that these questions about home get settled once we live for some time in a particular locale, adopt some protective coloration, learn to fit into the landscape, but in fact we may never resolve the issue.

In the West and in Alaska I got to realize all my dreams of hunting and fishing and exploring wild places. I moved to Alaska in 1964 and discovered that Alaska is like Montana writ large, an enormous difference of scale but not of kind. Westerners frequently survive better in Alaska than do many others. Despite this, and despite the fact that I had a wonderful and productive time, Alaska never became home in anything like the sense that Montana was. For years, when people in Alaska asked where I was from, I would answer Montana. The answer was true since that was my previous stop along the way, but what surprised me was the recognition, much later, that Iowa never occurred to me as another appropriate answer.

I went to Alaska, to the village of Naknek, as an exile, escaping the consequences of a divorce and looking for adventure. The former was impossible, of course, but the latter I found in abundance. As I talked to others it seemed that the people who moved to Alaska were one of two types: they were either escapists or opportunists. I was both. For a couple of years I told myself that the move was temporary. But Alaska has a way of getting its hooks into you. There is so much to learn, and one always starts from a base of incredible ignorance. None of the definitions that we live with so comfortably down here held true up there. There were profound cultural differences between Athapaskan, Eskimo, Aleut, and other Native groups, but the differences between their ways and our own were even greater than those among themselves.

Though political correctness was not an issue at that time, one did not wish to live among Native peoples and give offense, and one did not wish to live in a culture that was incomprehensible or in a territory where an unwitting offense against the nature of the land could cost you your life. Once I began to understand at least a bit of the culture and the world around me, my involvement in the life of the state increased. Like the rest of the American West, there is enough to learn in Alaska to keep one busy for more than a lifetime.

What puzzled me after a few years was that no matter how

much I learned or how involved I got, I still felt like an exile. That feeling never went away. What I came to understand during my second year in Naknek was that there are certain cultural barriers that one cannot cross. We are all human, and we all share certain human characteristics: the whole range of joy, grief, pain, suffering, and desire—all those great abstractions that play themselves out in our lives in very concrete ways every day. Yet our worldviews may be very different and more deep-seated than we realize.

I could have stayed in Naknek for the rest of my life. I could have learned the vestigial remnants of the local language that were still in use. I could have hunted and fished and trapped with the men and participated in the local cultural activities and learned as much about the place as it was possible to know. But when I was eighty I still would not see the world the way an Eskimo does. I was too immersed in my own scientifically bent, warped, twisted culture to develop a less skeptical and more thoughtful or accepting view of life and the world that seemed to me to characterize the village people I got to know in Naknek and all across the state.

When world oil prices collapsed in 1986, the Alaskan economy, primarily dependent on North Slope oil revenues, fell to pieces. Budget cuts, layoffs, foreclosures, and bankruptcies were common. There was a bitter joke that we had finally accomplished something: the number of bankruptcies had risen to equal the number of divorces. A largely artificial economy, propped up temporarily by increased capital expenditures for public buildings, collapsed along the fault lines we had created. Construction jobs were not the only ones that were lost. As one economist said in a public meeting in Anchorage in 1988, "There's no point in retraining folks to be hamburger flippers. Nobody's hiring hamburger flippers either."

Thousands of Alaskans had lived in the state for years, as far back as territorial days, and their children had never lived anywhere else. They called Alaska home. But the economy got so tight that many of those Alaskans sat down to dinner one night and said, "Honey, maybe we should go back home." When they heard what they had said, a kind of wonder came into their voices. Where was home, after all?

One way we distinguish the native from the stranger, the new-comer from the oldtimer, is by his or her knowledge of the names and stories of a place. Often a name implies a story or a particular knowledge of the region. Coming to know the names and the stories is partly a function of time. Nobody knows them all, but the longer one lives in a place, the more one hears.

The oldtimer gives directions that begin, "Well, you go down to the old Schneider place and turn west." The newcomer doesn't know which farm is the old Schneider place. How could he? It's been owned by the Seifkers, the Wentzels, and the Lowrys since Sam Schneider had it. He may recognize the Schneiders's weathered log barn with its gray hip roof when he goes by the next time, but he won't know the stories about the Schneiders, at least for a while. Of course, that one son of Sam's was worth talking about, and the greenhorn'll hear about him soon enough.

Here in the West I think I can distinguish the oldtimers from the newcomers, those who belong from those who don't, even those whose knowledge or ideas are apt to be trustworthy from those whose notions are apt to be ill-informed or foolish, by whether or not they know the story of Hugh Glass and the grizzly. Anybody who knows the West and loves it knows that story.

Glass was a trapper, already old, who headed West with Ash-ley to take part in the first fur trade expedition. While out hunt-ing for the party, he was mauled by a bear and so seriously torn up that Ashley left two men behind to watch over him while he died. Both men were fearful of Indians and wary of bears, so fi-nally they took Glass's gun and knife and left him to die alone. On their return to Ashley's party, they lied and told the men that

Hugh had expired and that they had given him a proper burial. Glass, however, did not die but dragged his broken bones and torn flesh two hundred miles over the prairie to find help, kept alive by berries, bugs, weeds, and a fierce desire for revenge. After resting up through the winter, he set out to find the men who had abandoned him and stolen his equipment. He eventually found them, but instead of killing them he simply reclaimed his gun and forced them to admit their culpability. Then he took off again into the wilderness on his own. He died with two companions seven years later when one of them struck a spark for a fire and it landed in a keg of gunpowder.

The best stories become part of personal and communal memory and then seem to grow from the land itself. What is absent from the stranger's view of the local landscape that would give it depth is memory. The visitor who is new to the Red Lodge country looks at Mount Maurice and sees a shapely form, the spruce that crowd the middle slopes, grassy meadows on the flanks below the dark trees. Depending on the month, the colors are mostly green in various shades, or black-green and beige if it's July or later.

The longtime Red Lodge resident looks at Mount Maurice and sees the same meadow as the newcomer, but memory and local knowledge reveal what is invisible to one who is new to the mountain: the meadows on the lower slopes where Crow Indians used to winter; the marks made by the travois on which they hauled their gear; the clearing where Bill Gams and Vin Eckerberg, a couple of Forest Service seasonals, on horseback, once tried to rope a black bear, acting out an old Charlie Russell painting; the stage road around the mountain's flank that marks the trail to Meeteetse, Wyoming; that other trail, invisible from the highway, that goes up the flank of the mountain from behind Piney Dell; the time the packhorse fell backward on that last really steep stretch near the top and should have broken his neck but never even broke a leg or scattered a pack; the low alluvial fan on the Clarks Fork side where Vern Waples found the bulwark thrown up and the spent brass cartridges lying behind it; the elk that range along the high meadows and the timberline on Sheridan Creek; the Line Creek Plateau behind the mountain where George Engler and Harv Schroeder went cat hunting for three days at temperatures ranging downward from a high of 25 below. Before he left, George's wife gave him a gunnysack. When he asked what it was for, she said, "So when things get bad, you can crawl inside and we won't have to look all over the mountain for your bones come spring." Those stories, and others, inform the viewing of anyone who knows the place.

But knowing the terrain—even knowing the stories and the culture and making lifelong friends—may not be sufficient to allow one to feel at home. Time, I've come to believe, is also critical. The time that is important here is not simply the number of years we spend in a place but the time we sense as we think about the past, a geologic time: How far can we go back into geologic time? Is there a paleontology of home? Montana got into me so deeply, in part at least, because of a sense of geologic roots. No matter how far back I go there—before the mountain men, before the Cheyennes, clear back past the paleolithic and past the dinosaurs to the oldest rocks anyone has yet identified—somehow, I'm still at home in a place I know. In Alaska I didn't have to go very far back until I hit something as impenetrable as permafrost, hard and alien, a feeling that I was no longer in my place but a stranger who had wandered far from where he *belonged*. That feeling is the difference between home and not-home. In Montana I am comfortable even in hard places; in Alaska I was uncomfortable even when I'd expected to feel at ease.

Not only the depth of knowledge, then, or the strength of friendships or the ties of memory, but how deeply one can go back in time seems to be a factor in finding a homeland, at least for me. That sense of the necessity of time in order to feel at home, and the sense that I can go as far back in time as I can imagine without displacement, has never changed for me.

Why is any of this important? Because if the West is home, not only for me but for others too, then it becomes crucial for all of us, newcomers and oldtimers alike, not to further foul a nest that is becoming increasingly crowded. Homeland—not some canyonland escape or playground but homeland—is our primary human sacred space, and it deserves the best attention we can give to its care.

If the past is close to us and the future is pressing in, perhaps we should think about what we've relearned in the past forty years. One of the facts we've learned anew is the connectedness of things, the idea that "all things are related," a refrain from an old Lakota song. That is not new knowledge. The knowledge that everything is connected is found in our oldest knowings, but we seem to have forgotten it for a time, maybe a few hundred years, maybe a thousand or more. Marcus Aurelius, the old Roman general, sat in his tent one night writing in his journal, reminding himself of that idea, which was not new with him:

> Always think of the universe as one living organism, with a single substance and a single soul; and observe how all things are submitted to the single perceptivity of this one whole, all are moved by its single impulse, and all play their part in the causation of every event that happens. Remark the intricacy . . . the complexity.

Beyond mere connectedness is the sense that damage to any one part will damage the whole, that if we destroy any element, we may unwittingly destroy ourselves. This is ancient knowledge not just in our culture but in many. There is a saying from the Aztecs: "The frog does not drink up the pond in which he lives." Today we have ample evidence that the Aztecs were right and that frogs may be smarter than we are.

In the midst of shrill rhetoric from every interest group, those of us who care about the West have to watch our language, keep our words clear. If the West is where a man's word is his bond, then we have to think about how we talk about things.

Until we get our language straight, we cannot get our stories about the West straight. Until we get our stories straight, we will never find the West as home. Home is where you can trust the story you are told, at least after you learn to recognize a tall tale. In a recent panel discussion Bill Kittredge said, "You cannot build a viable culture on the basis of half-truths, outright lies, and expurgated stories. In the West we've been trying to do just that, and it is not working. We need to tell ourselves a new story about the West."

That new story may be shaped by the past. Walter Rosenberry—a Denver philanthropist, teacher, and friend—talked to me once about Samuel Sewell, a seventeenth-century Puritan who hated slavery and fought against it. Walter told me that Sewell, in thinking about blacks, wrote, "We should accord them a respect agreeable." Like Walter, I love that phrase. It applies to so much more than our attitude toward other races or cultures or genders. It's appropriate for all of us who love our homeland and want to see it persist in the face of numerous assaults upon it.

To accord our western lands a respect agreeable, to accord the rivers of the West, the cities of the West, our everyday discourse, and our public rhetoric a respect agreeable—those are tasks worthy of westerners. They are tasks that will lead to a new story about the West, a story about respect, a story that all of us creatures can live with. When we can accord the West and every place else a respect agreeable, we may discover that we can respect ourselves as well and may find that we are home at last.

RIVERS

I've known rivers, ancient dusky rivers.
My soul has grown deep, like the rivers.

—Langston Hughes

Inside each of us a river runs, perhaps more than one. For me there are at least two. One is small: Elk Creek flows indelibly through my childhood in northeast Iowa among hills too steep to plow or use for pasture. There are trees on the hills, fed by the creek: walnut, oak, hickory, an occasional ironwood, linden, or maple. There are raspberries, red and black, and currants. In summer, watercress chokes the smaller tributaries, and in fall sumac flares brilliant in the undergrowth. Elk Creek runs clear and cool and, unusual in the Midwest, has rainbow trout that could be caught on a fly rod using single salmon eggs.

Among my earliest memories are images of picnics, all of us in the old Ford, driving down the dirt road past the Spring Creek Mill, built in 1867, its huge wooden wheel still turning in the creek in my childhood. I remember riding on the wagon's high seat with my grandfather as we took the team and wagon down to the mill to get yellow corn ground into meal. He took me upstairs to see the great hand-hewn limestone wheels turning almost imperceptibly. Along Elk Creek near a wooden bridge we would spread blankets under the trees to eat. It was cool under the great trees even in August, when the Iowa nights were so hot we could hear the corn grow, and there were squirrels to hunt in October when the leaves were aflame with approaching death. I still believe that those October days of squirrel hunting among the trees along Elk Creek were some of the finest days of my life.

The other river is huge. The Mississippi flows below the bluffs at Dubuque, Iowa, where I was raised, through Lock and Dam Number 11. A few miles above Dubuque, the great river stretches nearly a mile across the widest point it carves on its way to the Gulf of Mexico. Ostensibly built for flood control, the dams flooded thousands of acres that had never been flooded before. We called it "the best dammed river in the world." That river still runs in me, somewhere. The first time I went duck hunting with my father, when I was about ten, we stood on its sloughy banks in willows higher than my head, holding shot-guns. There were plenty of ducks—thousands of them along this stretch of the Mississippi flyway—but the day was too nice, the ducks flying too high. Occasionally a single would cross our line of sight in range, and I would watch, briefly mesmerized, as it sailed past. They appeared so suddenly, so unpredictably, and passed so quickly that it did not occur to me to shoot.

There may have been a third river. If I sound tentative about that, it is only because the third is not really a river but a flow of water along the curb on the street in front of our house. When I was five, or eight, dark thunder-and-lightning storms would be-siege the seven hills of Dubuque and we would go out in the street to play. The downpour would flood along the curb, the late afternoon sky to the west would flare with sheet lightning, and we would dam the river headed down to the iron gutters at the bottom of Bennett Street. Sometimes we carried rocks and gravel from the alley beside my house, but the easiest way was to lie down on one's side in the street and curl into a near fetal po-sition, with knees against the curb and body funneling the water against the tops of our thighs to pool between thigh and curb and belly and chest. The rain was so warm on those summer days that it could lull one to sleep right there in the street, thunder cracking as if in a dream. Latent in me still may reside an impulse, as Richard Hugo said, "to alter the river."

When I was seventeen, I used to walk, often at night and lonely, along a little stream near Hopkinton, Iowa. In winter on moonlit nights the bare, black branches of the trees moved suggestively in the slightest wind, making patterns against the moon, their shadows shifting on the silver water or on patches of snow along the bank. The stream then seemed full of mystery and solace, a pull so powerful, alive, and poignant that the river was wildly romantic, achingly erotic. Only women could have been more mysterious, elemental, and attractive. I wrote poems then that began, "The river is a woman / dressed in black lace." I had never seen a woman in black lace.

Once, standing in a riffle on the South Fork of the Shoshone in Wyoming, I dropped a Joe's Hopper on the quiet water just above me. As I watched, intent, a fish the size of a cottonwood trunk rose to the surface and the fly disappeared. I set the hook, but the fish did not run, did not need to; it could do whatever it pleased. What pleased it for a time was to settle back where it had been before. It did not seem to know it had my fly in its lip. I could not move it. I pulled carefully to my right and again to my left. I waited impatiently, then bumped the bottom of the rod with the heel of one hand. I had no net and was up against a high cutbank. I looked around for a spot to do something with this creature from the river, but there was no nearby place to land such a fish.

As the time passed I did not know whether to be frantic or bored, for the fish just sat there. I yanked on the line as I might if I'd had a snag, but it made no difference. I was tied to that fish, and the fish had a mind of its own, just sitting out there in the river. How can you catch something that doesn't even know it's been caught?

I moved cautiously on the slippery rocks, making my way toward the fish while also trying not to get water over the top of my boots. The fish, as if oblivious to the commotion I was making in the river, still did not move. Carefully, I reached down and pulled a rock from the river bottom. I threw it just beyond the place where my line entered the water. There was no response. I got close enough to see the dark form in the water. It looked as long as my leg and as heavy. I had never been connected to such a fish before. Finally, as if he were making a judgment after long deliberation, or perhaps because he sensed my presence or had tired of the pull on his lip, or was acting in response to a signal from a friend upstream, he began to move lazily against the current. I followed as best I could, keeping the line taut. He turned back and I grabbed frantically for line, then he suddenly began to run wildly across the river. He caught me unprepared, line tore from the spool, but we stayed together, bound by the river and the line, while he slashed around.

At last he began to drift back. I thought he was tired, but he was still upright in the water, keeping his head upstream. He came down close to my left leg but just out of reach. I could see his brightness then through the clear water, the fins working easily. Holding the rod high, trying in vain to horse him just a little closer, I reached down to slip my left hand into his gills. Perhaps he saw the shadow, perhaps I pulled too hard, but with a simple flip of his head he broke the leader and swam leisurely away, apparently not the least bit excited. I stumbled back, almost falling, legs shaking, hands trembling, then moved downstream to where I could finally get out and sit on the bank. There are things in the river beyond our human control.

The old poet might have said, "To those who in the love of rivers, hold communion with their visible forms, they speak a various language." He did not, but anyone who has known rivers knows that they do speak, that they offer many levels of discourse. The river, as Norman Maclean says in *A River Runs through It,* carries on a continual conversation with itself. Under the rocks of the river are the words, The Word—in the fly-fishing, Johanine, sense—the word that lies at the bottom of all creation. My rivers may be less theological, more personal, but the voice of Elk Creek, and the trees along its banks, have not diminished with age and distance.

I have no way of knowing what river or rivers flow in other people, but I suspect there is at least one. Your rivers and mine together become *the* river—not a faceless, generic river, but The River: Tigris, Euphrates, Platte, Mississippi, Bighorn, Nile, Niobrara, or Tongue, the Yellow, the Missouri, or the Yellowstone. The river is embedded in our souls not only because it has slaked our thirst and given life to the grain and game upon which we depend but also because our own human blood has been drained back into the river. We have absorbed rivers; we carry them in our living tissue, and they have absorbed us, carrying us in their spiraling currents and eddies. The blood of our ancestors, our kin, has seeped into the Rosebud, the Big Hole, and the Ganges, into Sand Creek, the Amazon, and the Orinoco, and their names ring in our minds and stir us still. "I've known rivers, . . ." wrote Langston Hughes, "My soul has grown deep, like the rivers."

We began in the sea or on its edge, and our bodies are mostly water. From the beginning we have been among the creatures who settle along the streams and lakes or on the nearby terraces above them. For a million years, perhaps even three million, we have generally not settled, or even stopped for the night, far from water. Our heritage is one of shore dwelling. Only in recent years have we been able to distance ourselves somewhat, been skilled enough to bring water to locations far removed from a river or lake in quantities sufficient to sustain large communities. We know the Babylonians did it, and their irrigated gardens are said to have been one of the Seven Wonders of the Ancient World. Unfortunately, they couldn't keep their ditches from silting up, and they could not sustain themselves. The Romans may have been the best at diverting and transporting water. We can still see parts of their great viaducts standing above the narrow valleys in central Italy and southern

France. But they could not control their politics and also were not able to sustain themselves.

It would seem that therein lie two clues to understanding what we must do to maintain our own culture: better understand the implications of our technology and discipline ourselves.

In our own country, as we left our forested East to move out onto the arid western savannas, rivers came to have a dual significance. We used them then not only to sustain us but also to transport us and our possessions. We followed the rivers in part because they were going our way (or coming our way) and in part because we couldn't leave them with any assurance that there would be water elsewhere. The sun was so persistent, the ground so dry, the storms so brief and fierce, that water ran off or soaked in before we could think to contain it. When we did stop and settle, we settled along a river.

So, somewhere in almost every western town that has survived there is a river. Sometimes it is hard to find—Denver's Cherry Creek is no longer the main feature of Cherry Creek, a shopping mall of upscale boutiques and espresso shops—though sometimes there is a small parkway along the banks, or a still-necessary bridge. Frequently, as in Santa Fe, the river is dry, the bottom concrete, the refuse and discards of town life more apparent than they should be. Most often the stream that meant life to the early community is now considered unimportant and insufficient, and the water that keeps the town growing comes from more distant places. Most residents can't tell you where.

Water or the lack of it, rivers or their absence, are among the defining characteristics of the West. People as knowledgeable and experienced as John Wesley Powell and Wallace Stegner have urged us to think of the West as arid land, and they were right to do so. What we know from our western past and our own present is that water is one of the critical resources, that in our region it tends to be scarce, and that it has been and is the focus of intense argument and debate, and sometimes the cause of violent confrontation and death. Thousands of homesteaders were defeated by the failure of rain to come. They believed what they had been told, that rain follows the plow, that rain is tied to settlement, and that as the West filled up with people, the rain would automatically increase. Surely such faith in rain, or such willingness to believe our fellow human hucksters, gives us ample reason to ask whether there is intelligent life on Earth.

Not everyone believed the booster story about water. Fearing that they would not have enough, some who had early rights to the river took it all and left none for their neighbors downstream. Mary Austin told a story about a man who sat on his headgate with a gun and warned off his neighbors who came to see what had happened to the water. When one downstream owner came armed, the man shot him five times in the chest. The next man to own the neighbor's plot was smarter. He sent his wife to the headgate in the middle of the night. She was a formidable woman of considerable size, and when the farmer came up in the morning to protect his water, she was sitting on the headgate knitting, a long-handled shovel across her lap and the water already turned into her husband's fields. The man, true to the code of the West, would not shoot a woman, and since she looked so strong and was armed with a shovel, he would not attack her one on one either.

Though it is dry, we are here, we say, because we love the West, especially its landscape. But if we love the West, we will beware of anyone who proposes to bring us an endless supply of bountiful water and will do everything we can to thwart the plan. If such a person were successful, it would mean the end of the West as we know it. That person brings us not a happy life in the West; he or she would bring us Ohio.

We remember our rivers even if we do not honor them. They enliven our sense of the past and inform our sense of the present. Driving on Interstate 80 across the southwestern corner of Wyoming, any westerner is reminded that about forty miles south of the highway, down on Henrys Fork, is the site of the first free trappers' rendezvous, held in 1825. A westerner also remembers that a little north of the highway, on the Green River, is the site of one of the last rendezvous, in 1835—such a short span to have such a mythic hold on the American imagination. Perhaps the strength of that image lies in the knowledge that nearly every incident in our western recollection of those days is connected with a river. Across Blacks Fork just south of the divided highway, one can see the location of Jim Bridger's old fort and trading post. It was a good site. The valley, even in high summer, is still a mild green in the midst of the desert gray and beige.

But memory is insufficient to keep the river flowing. If one continues along I-80, swinging down into Utah, the land drops off into Echo Reservoir. In late summer the reservoir is low and the east side is a long slope down to the water. The lower end is almost barren except for a trickle that drains into Echo River. These are apt names—both reservoir and river are but echoes of past water. What lures a fisherman there now, the memory of past fish? The men standing on either side of the Ford Bronco parked in the willows are so far away that one cannot actually see what they are doing, but memory fills in our knowledge. By their intent posture one knows that these men have fishing rods crooked inside their arms. They have just threaded line through the guides and are knotting leader or monofilament. In a few seconds a hand will grasp the invisible rod, holding it next to a thigh, almost horizontal to the ground, tip raised slightly. Then the left leg will lift to step toward the path through the soft willows to the headwaters of Echo River. No need to practice prophecy to see the future here; it is revealed by memory. For the rest, to answer the question of whether they will catch any fish, one can be as fancifully imaginative as any novelist or historian. One of those men will hook a fish so big it will drag him down the creek, through the canyon, and into the Great Salt Lake. Tomorrow, searchers will find only his hat floating toward Antelope Island, and he will dwell in the house of the lake forever.

If the river stirs our fantasies, it is neither memory nor fancy but reality that tells us that the river is our parent. It was here before we were; in its soft lilt we were born. The river nourished us when we were new on the earth and sustained us as we grew. But like all parents the river is growing old as we grow older. Now, as sometimes happens with our own aging parents, the roles are reversed and the life of the river is in our hands. We must care for it as once it cared for us.

Though water has been one of the most complex and divisive issues in the West, it is also what draws us together in this place and allows us to stay. Water is the common bond that we share with one another and with all other creatures. It is one of the gifts that we have to have in order to live and that we therefore must share. Historically, if there has been any healing in the world, it has come from the rivers. It is "by the rivers of Babylon that we lay ourselves down, by the cooling waters we lay down." Water is not only a difficult, complex, and divisive issue; it is a source of our unity, a symbol of rest and health for mind and body, and our great hope.

SIGNS OF HOPE

Start with Seattle. I am about to leave, but first I head down Second Avenue toward Pioneer Square, an urban renewal project from the sixties still popular in these early nineties. It is the home of the Elliott Bay Book Company, arguably the best bookstore in the West and one of the best anywhere, and I need some books to take with me on this trip. A couple of blocks from the square, five or six homeless men are huddled in an alcove. As I approach, one man starts yelling "Get him!" and suddenly all of the men are facing into the dark doorway yelling, pushing, kicking, and stomping. I think that perhaps a man is down in there and I stop, but as the melee slows and the arms and feet stop flying I see that they have cornered a huge rat, its pale gray belly and darker back now bloody and lifeless. One man reaches down to grab its tail and swings the carcass around his head and out into the street, everyone laughing and whooping and breathing hard after their exertion.

Stocked up with books, I escape from Seattle this late fall evening at about 8:30, heading up over Snoqualmie Pass in my little Dodge Caravan. It has been raining for days and the valleys north of Seattle are flooding, but the rain is slowing now and the moon is breaking through. The curve on the lesser side of this five-eighths moon is exquisitely sensual, suspended in the clearing night like a communion wafer. "Oh, silver majesty of night, Moon," says Faust from his dark study. I peer ahead through the windshield at mountain slopes that appear silvery, as if covered by ice. But it is not cold enough for ice, even up here, and it finally sinks in that I am looking at rainwater running off the clear-cut hills in silver sheets. The clear-cuts are ugly in the evening light, and I am forced to acknowledge that the country has not come back despite claims of reforestation. Yet the stumps and slash on the slopes are less ugly than the logging roads bladed across the face of the mountains, a gravel wound not to be healed in my time, nor in my children's. The homeless in the city and the wounded countryside drive me to look for signs of hope. I pull into Pendleton in northeastern Oregon at about 12:30 A.M., wake the patient motel man that I have wakened before, and stop for the night.

Oregon offers a rich context for considering some of the common issues westerners face. It provides a link to the myth of the past and reveals what many westerners now confront in their cities, towns, and countryside. Oregon was once the Shangri-la at the end of the long, exhausting, westward trail and became home to many retired mountain men and trappers at the end of their sad journeying after the colorful days of mythmaking were over.

Upon his arrival in Portland in 1840, Joe Meek, the Merry Mountain Man who nearly lost his life more than once, put up in a hotel and ordered dinner in its restaurant. When told that there was no wild game on the menu, he reluctantly agreed to sample the beef. Allowing that it was not too bad, he said, "That'll do. Fetch me four pounds of the same." He stayed on to become a U.S. marshall. Osborne Russell, who knew Meek from their old trapping days and who had worked with Jim Bridger as well, wrote the best journal of those free-trapper days yet discovered. He became a respected judge in Oregon and ran for public office. Now the myths of those wild early days have withered as scholars have shone more of the light of reality on the history and environment of the West and as people turn to consider the contemporary issues we all confront.

My trip is part of a series of travels in eight states: Montana, Wyoming, Colorado, Utah, Idaho, and the eastern parts of Washington, Oregon, and Nevada. As a field representative for the National Endowment for the Humanities, I am looking for ways in which scholars might work with local citizens on questions of mutual interest. In order to do that I need to know what local citizens are thinking. The most important part of my work, therefore, is listening to people talk about themselves and their communities. But listening to people is a way of getting acquainted not just with individuals but with an entire countryside. People's voices sooner or later reveal their character, and many of them taken together sketch the characteristics of a region.

Many western communities face difficult choices about their future. Most of their concerns have a history, a context, which, if known, may make better choices possible. Every concern has ethical implications, and a philosopher who is trained in ethics can occasionally help local citizens see alternatives that might not be apparent to an untrained eye. My job is to try to bring scholars together with folks who don't normally have access to them in hope that our citizens can make wiser choices about their common present and future.

The people I meet in small western towns are frequently open, willing to talk, and candid about their hopes and fears, and most have lively, thoughtful minds. Listening to them is most often a privilege, for the conversations are frequently intense and create a rewarding intimacy. Such listening requires a great deal of concentration, but if I listen carefully and have done my homework, perhaps I can suggest a historian, a writer, an anthropologist, an economist, a philosopher, or a linguist who has dealt with such matters before or has studied them carefully. Such a person might be willing to come to meet with local folks or even provide the core for a conference about their concerns. I can also help find funds through state humanities councils and other sources to make such events happen. When everything comes together, as it would later in Springdale, Utah, everybody—scholars and local folks alike—learns something.

Over the years I have sat in on more than two hundred meetings, met hundreds of people in small towns and waysides throughout the region, and seen some of America's most open, beautiful, and demanding country. This is a story of the land and of conversations with people that I met while traveling in three small towns in eastern Oregon (with a couple of side trips thrown in). I can report that no part of the West is at ease, but I can also report that there are signs of hope.

Here's one: Nearly every small town I visited has a cadre of concerned citizens willing to devote considerable effort to making their community a healthier and happier place for everyone.

Here's another: In many small towns the sense of place and of community, although diminished, is still very much alive. People are working to increase or bring back a definition of community that includes a more just and humane society. They are urgent in their desire to create a real home—a place of safety, comfort, and pride—for themselves, their children, and their neighbors. Such citizens get scant attention in the newspapers; many people do not even know they exist. But there are lots of folks out there in towns large and small thinking hard about how to contribute to the community and make it a better place.

Everywhere I went in the West people were concerned about the economy—no surprise—but they fretted about more than their personal economies. Those who cared about their communities, and that was most people, worried about the ability of their small towns to survive, about how retail store owners could hang on long enough to escape defeat, or how loggers or ranchers could survive the failings of their industries. But everyone knows that the economy is tough, and urban tenement dwellers experience that fear and frustration as strongly as people in small towns and out in the country.

What caught my attention were three additional concerns that ranked right up there with the economy—close enough in the minds of many to be inseparable. One of those concerns was schools: Throughout the West, communities large and small were worried about their schools. The second, nearly equivalent concern was people's failure to participate in community events, a withdrawal from public life. The third was a resurgence of racial or ethnic tensions, now becoming increasingly overt. None of these concerns is unique to the West, but that is where I encountered them, and the West is one of the places that must learn to deal with them.

"We don't understand what the schools are trying to do anymore," one woman began. She was sitting on a gray folding chair in the basement of Pendleton's busy, popular town library. Folks here worry about their schools, and unlike small western towns where the economy is the primary frustration, people I talked to mentioned them first. Another woman expanded on the previous speaker's idea: "The teachers feel that no one is behind them. There are lots of educational workshops for teachers, way more work days than there used to be, but we don't know what teachers do with them."

The women hail from Pendleton, but as far as they know, their feelings are new. People sound bemused, almost surprised, that they are giving voice to such notions, for they clearly want to believe in their schools. Yet in the early 1990s the cost of their schools was rising almost as rapidly as health costs, they say, and they do not know why. It isn't so much that schools are doing a bad job, though the media make as much of that news here as they do elsewhere, but that parents just don't understand what is happening in their schools anymore, don't know what the purpose of education is even though they go to parent-teacher conferences and PTA meetings and know their children's teachers by their first names. Here, as elsewhere, the scores on standardized tests are falling, too many students drop out, too many don't seem to have adequate skills to fit into the workforce, too many don't seem as well equipped for the world as previous generations even though they may know "lots of stuff I never learned," as one parent put it. She went on to say, "Motivation is missing, maybe. We *knew* we had to work!"

Drugs and child abuse are also concerns and are related to a perception that new people are moving in. In referring to these problems one woman said, "The demographics are changing. Just talk to a judge. Anybody who's served on a jury knows." This was a contention I also ran into elsewhere in the West, a sense that the ground is shifting, that the rules have been changed, that no one is certain just what the rules are anymore. In the view of many, the shift had to do with newcomers—the new minorities, the fantastically rich who are buying up western real estate, and the drifting poor who depend on state or county welfare. New people are often perceived as a threat rather than an asset. "They do not know or respect the town's ways," a woman says, "and they don't do anything to learn them."

One person in this small group in the Pendleton library worries about an issue that strikes directly at the future of democracy, or the loss of it: "People are burned out about everything," she says. "It's really hard to get anyone to come out to anything." A neighbor of hers continues: "It's not just that people don't go to church anymore. They don't come to Rotary or Chamber. They don't go to school board or city council. They just go home at night and turn on the TV."

These women's observations have been reinforced recently by the work of such social scientists as Robert Putnam, who outlines the decline of both trust and participation in American life, noting that they have declined 20 to 30 percent in the last couple of decades. He carefully demolishes most of the reasons given for our lack of trust and chalks up the withdrawal to television. That may be true enough, but another explanation for our loss of trust and our failure to take part in public life may be found in other comments I heard as well: People simply believe that their institutions have lied to them and are no longer worthy of trust.

"Why should we trust them?" one articulate man asked. "The Vatican muzzles priests who try seriously to serve the poor. TV evangelists are doing time in the federal pen for fraud. Our state university is facing lawsuits for sexual harassment and for ignoring minority faculty in their hiring and advancement practices. Neither Democrats or Republicans seem capable of meeting a campaign promise or keeping their skirts clean. Every time you invest yourself in party politics or in working on behalf of kids, you get burned."

Mike Hyde is a tall, lean, slow-talking man who has been in Pendleton as city planner for twelve years and who is eager to get some new census data. But the trends, I suggest, probably won't change much, will they? "Probably not," he says, "but the new information is always fun to read." He retrieves some pages from the Pendleton Comprehensive Plan, marks some places on the map, and gives me a little bundle of material. I get a somewhat different impression from him than from the folks I met the night before. Their sense that the demographics are shifting in some vaguely alarming way doesn't seem to be borne out by Mike's experience, "at least not by the statistics in our comp plan," he says.

The new state penitentiary, he tells me, is housed in a remodeled mental hospital. It seems to work fine for medium-security inmates and, he says, "It was far cheaper to remodel the hospital than to build new." The new facility confines about 1,800 prisoners, whose sentences average nine months. "That makes the time too brief for many prisoner families to move from Seattle or Portland to Pendleton, so we haven't had many of them move in."

I mention the public perception of an influx, a vaguely threatening change in the demographics of the region. He shakes his head no, considers a moment, then acknowledges the possibility with, "Well, the census data don't show it, but the Salvation Army was complaining their resources were being strained a while back."

In a brochure I picked up, Pendleton's Umatilla County brags that it spends only 10 percent of its tax dollars on human services while spending 17.1 percent on tax assessment and collection. Here, as elsewhere in the West, *human services* translates as *welfare* and is seen by many as a scam. The myth of western self-sufficiency, or at least self-reliance, is still strong here. But it is, and always has been, a fatuous notion. The West, historians like William Cronon, Richard White, and Elliott West are showing us with evidence that is overwhelming, has been utterly dependent on the federal government and major cities back east since the approval of the U.S. Constitution. Yet the myth persists, nourishing the egos of those who make it in this culture and killing the sensibility of those who don't. In our western myth, there is something wrong with people who don't make it, a lack of sturdiness, of spirit, of git-go—in short, a lack of character, a moral lack that ought not to be encouraged by giving people welfare. Such feelings are especially powerful in towns like Pendleton where people cherish their western heritage and, despite pursuing their urban enterprises, continue to support the rodeo, wear high-heeled boots, and sport big hats.

At Halfway, southeast of Pendleton and almost to the Idaho line, Dick Lewis, the director of the Oregon Humanities Council, is showing a film at the community center and museum, a brief documentary called *The Stonecarvers,* about the lives of immigrant Italian stonecarvers working on the National Cathedral in Washington, D.C. It includes footage of their work and of conversations among them about their carving traditions and the master teachers they worked with as apprentices in the Old Country. About fifty citizens have come to see the film and talk with Dick and me about their community. Here, as in many western towns regardless of size, is a little cadre of people who want to keep their community stimulating, whose own intellectual curiosity is keen, and who persist in their efforts to enliven the place for everyone.

As Dick was rewinding the film, a local man stood up and said, "This is a kindergarten-level film. It just gives the surface, but it very carefully avoids questions like what is in the stone and what the carver can bring out of the stone. This is kindergarten stuff. It doesn't raise important questions like what's important about gargoyles is their mass. It doesn't matter what the face or figure looks like. They are put in the buttress, and their mass is a shock absorber for the buttress and the wall." He's not a tactful fellow, but he is an interesting one, someone who has learned to play his role, and from the expression on the faces of other participants I'd bet he does it at every public meeting. He probably sees himself as the devil's advocate of Halfway's intelligentsia, or maybe the only member of its intelligentsia. Dick handled him very well. "One good thing about films like this," he said, "is that they are short. Not everything can be said, but they give you room in a discussion to develop ideas. It stimulates thinking about other directions than the film can take you."

We soon learned that the status of the schools is worrisome here too, as are development issues. This town has always depended on agriculture. It is an idyllic, bucolic, riparian farming enclave in the midst of some of the West's most arid country. Here the hay is a mix of purple clover, timothy, and rye grass, as opposed to that on irrigated land over the hill, which is alfalfa. Important as agriculture is to the community, and unique as Halfway's agriculture is in this arid country, one woman notes that "I've been in agriculture all my life, and in eight years of school my son has never heard the word *agriculture.*"

Recently Halfway has been discovered, and now wealthy Californians are buying up chunks of property, driving real estate values up, creating a pattern that is clearly discernible in other communities around the West. Ultimately, inflated real estate prices, and the expensive homes that will be built on the real estate, will drive up the assessed value of the land, taxes will get uncomfortably high, and old established families will have a hard time hanging on to their places. The marginal subsistence they have depended on won't yield enough cash to cover the increased cost of ownership. They'll either sell out and move to a place that is less expensive or simply lose their home to pay the taxes. Local residents will then become members of the service economy, working at minimum wage and driving forty miles to work from a trailer park that new zoning ordinances will prohibit as a low-income eyesore. They can't quite see that yet, but without careful preparations or blind luck, it will come.

Just now, logging is in decline, agriculture is as tough as ever, and tourism is untested over the long haul. The town can't decide which future it wants to cultivate, and many folks resist the changes. Here too the demographics are changing, and here too the schools seem out of touch with local realities.

A couple of months after my first trip, I head for Halfway again. South of Baker a hawk glides steeply, tucks its wings, plummets straight down, hits the ground so hard she bounces, sits up in the short grass, and looks around as if she's embarrassed and wants to see if anyone is watching. Sure enough, thirty-five yards off a coyote has been watching it all from his seat on a ditch bank, head cocked to one side quizzically, about to make some smart-ass coyote comment.

From Baker the road winds eastward up into dry hills, crossing the old Oregon Trail, its ruts still visible. The country finally lifts to a high divide, the Wallowa Mountains, home to the Nez Percé. This region of high, rolling hills, arid and brown now, is exciting because it seems remote, hidden, off the beaten track. That is part of its appeal to wealthy folks from distant cities. As I drive up the bottom of the little canyon of the Powder River, the sky turns abruptly dark and the Powder turns too, from translucent green to slate black. Coming out of the canyon west of Richland, I see there are two golden eagles on the bank of the river, wings extended, shoulders humped over as they tear at something in the grass.

From the ridge above Halfway one looks east out over a lovely basin—a "hole" in the mountains, the free trappers would have called it. From here I can see a squall across the valley, reaching down to obscure the mountains. Rain falls in dark streaks, driving down on a ranch nestled in a coulee at the mountain's base. The rest of the valley is clear.

I've asked a few folks in Halfway to meet with me so that we can continue the discussion begun by Dick Lewis. Half a dozen people are waiting at the newspaper office when I arrive. Lest anyone think such towns lack sophistication or are out of touch with the rest of the world, take note: These folks can travel, and they do. They supplement the news with memories of places the news reports come from. Since we last met, Donna Higgins has been to Juneau, Alaska, for ten days. Donna Hammar has spent a month in Europe. Steve Backstrom had planned to travel but has been chained to his desk because two staffers at the newspaper recently quit and have not been replaced. I find him in the darkroom and we go over to Wild Bill's for coffee.

This day everyone is a bit down and dispirited. "You got me on a down day," says Steve. "Donna Hammar and I were just talking about how nobody comes to our Cornucopia Arts Council events. We're always losing money." There are two Donnas here, and Donna Higgins looks a bit depressed too. "People buy concert series tickets to Baker and drive sixty-five miles over there but don't come to good stuff here," she says. "Even teachers won't come. We had a scholar who does a one-man show as Yeats in town, but not a single teacher came. We had a one-woman show about Emily Dickinson, but nobody from the school showed up. Retired folks are another big group that doesn't come." The problem here, as Donna Higgins said, is not that people don't want to attend a concert or a play but that they slight good ones in their own town to attend others far away. The assumption seems to be that if it happens in Halfway, it can't be as good as an event that happens somewhere else.

Melanie Cracker, who does massage and works on the newspaper, and her friend Mary Jo are typical of many young westerners who cobble up their income from several sources and settle for less because they want to live in a place that is so special in many ways. She throws the theme onto a larger screen: "It is always the same folks who come, and the community is so split, and the atmosphere so stultifying. If it isn't bluegrass, nobody comes. Or people come by interest groups. You may get the loggers for one event, the ranchers for another, but nobody comes to the other person's event. They label stuff right away: 'Oh, that's for miners,' and then no one else comes." The doldrums don't last, however, and the conversation expands as they consider how to pull together a community that is fragmented and indifferent and that appears to have a "Can any good thing come out of Nazareth/Halfway?" self-image.

These folks not only travel, they also read good books. Donna Hammar is curious about Dan Kemmis. Carol Bly, she notes, has done some good writing on community. They think maybe a tie with the American Association of University Women in Baker and Eastern Oregon State College in La Grande would make a nice three-part lecture series. They speculate that Kemmis, Bly, and perhaps Oregon novelist Craig Leslie or Montana fiction writer and essayist Bill Kittredge might come to speak. Their enthusiasm seems to be rebounding at the prospect of such leaven to lift their community spirit, but the prospects for attendance are bleak. They want to bridge some of the fractures in their community and believe that they can if they find the right draw. "But what if we gave a party with guests like that and no one came?" someone asks. This time, instead of becoming submerged in gloom, everyone laughs.

After the meeting I drift across the street to the Stockman's, a local bar and cafe, for a bowl of soup. As I sit down, a county sheriff's deputy rises to leave and stops to talk to a family in a booth nearby. The boy, about ten, is fascinated by the police gear, runs his fingers over the handcuffs, reaches to touch the gun. The deputy says no to that, turns his hip away. But he cannot help puffing up a bit at the rapt attention, a real Don Knotts move, and he walks with a different gait going out the door.

One of the things I've been told is that people in this valley know nothing of the outside world. Donna and Donna, and others too, give the lie to such an idea, but here in the cafe an older man seems determined to prove it true. Thin and gray-haired, with white stubble on his face, he is holding forth at the next table. He seems to want to let his friends know that he is a man of wide experience. "Went to a big Greek dinner in Albuquerque one time," he says. "It was wonderful. Afterwards this guy I was with said he didn't know a thing he ate, but he liked it. Somebody told us not a single thing had been cooked; it was all raw. The Greeks do that. It takes weeks for a big holiday dinner, soaking things in spices and getting ready. You won't recognize a thing when you eat it, but it will be good. The Greeks do that." Later he notes the ten-year-old pleading with his parents to buy him something and comments, "When I was a kid, we hadda make everything, all our toys—rubber guns, darts. We could shoot darts clear outta sight. Hadda make all our own stuff. Nobody had any money to buy nothing. There wasn't any money. . . . Slingshots, yeah. Some people call 'em slingshots, but slingshots yuh swing around yer head. These were like bean shooters. Nigger shooters I always called 'em. That's what we all called 'em—nigger shooters."

On the way back to Baker a flock of ducks sets their wings to settle on Eagle Creek, then suddenly flares, scatters and lifts to get away, but I cannot see what warned them off. There are three signs in the window of the Richland filling station, one above the other:

Ice Cream
Soda Pop
Nightcrawlers

A young man, sixteen or seventeen, comes out to pump gas, a service mandated by law in Oregon and one I have a hard time remembering. I ask the young man if he wants to recommend one or the other of the snacks advertised on the signs in his window. He deadpans, "Nooo, but I can make your choice easier. . . . We're outta nightcrawlers."

In ways that may be hard for people in more settled regions to understand, in the West land is still an abiding, occasionally overwhelming presence. Wherever we travel, the land sweeps out before us and views of thirty miles, even a hundred miles or more, are common. In towns like Pendleton we look up from our desks and between the buildings of downtown businesses we see the sere hills and sense anew the distance and the vistas, the history and the stories that still make the West exciting even as its urban areas continue to expand. Every rancher knows that there are still remote canyons where no one is apt to come along for days.

Ontario, Oregon, in the southeast corner of the state near the Idaho border, is to all appearances a thriving business community with an agricultural base, but now it too is under pressure. Poor markets, a lack of water, and shifting demographics all play a role in the changes that are taking place. "Some folks have been building for a lifetime. Now it's all disappearing," one man says in a get-together at Treasure Valley Community College. "It's sort of a joke," another says, "but loggers and ranchers are saying, 'Maybe we should get ourselves put on that endangered species list.'" The issues are serious enough that three towns in the area—Nyssa, Vail, and Ontario—pulled together a planning committee. They had already done some surveys and had determined that "appearance" was a primary concern for all three places and that "a positive multi-cultural life together" was another. Some people indicated that the Hispanics, the Japanese, the American Indians, and the Anglos don't mix much. "There's maybe a lack of a sense that we're in this together, too little sense of community," one woman said.

At the community college I visit Dale Haynes, whose office is in the college library. She is the grantsperson for the college, and we talk a bit about Ontario, its ethnic makeup, and other demographic information. While Dale takes a phone call, I browse through the county's latest census report, then we walk down to meet Cathy Maeda, the college's public information director.

On the way Dale tells me that there really is not much sharing of culture between the ethnic groups here in town or around Malheur County, not much cross-fertilization: "We don't go to their Cinco de Mayo. They don't come to our symphony," she says. I suggest that maybe she could get the symphony to build a concert entirely around Hispanic classical music, a whole evening of Falla, Villa-Lobos, or Celtic Spain. Advertise it as a Hispanic program. Show both Anglos and Hispanics the classic side of what is often dismissed as a simple folk culture. Structure a whole concert around an idea—not a musical idea but a community idea. You could even do it with religious music: Catholic sacred music from chant to mass, for instance, or shape-note congregational singing instead of a standard oratorio. Japanese music, with its wondrous strings and percussion instruments, and some Anglo composers deeply influenced by it could make up another evening. Dale shrugs, "We couldn't get our symphony to do that."

Cathy Maeda was raised here. Her grandparents were Japanese interred here during the war, an event that has colored all their lives since. When I was there in 1991, an effort was underway to establish a Japanese heritage museum with some of the reparations money that Congress had recently granted in acknowledgment of the loss of businesses, land, and income the Japanese had suffered due to internment. But older Japanese were fearful that the publicity such an effort would entail could re-ignite the racial animosity they had felt in the forties. Cathy tells us, "'No, no,' they say fearfully, as if shushing a child who might awaken ghosts. 'Don't talk about that.'"

Sure enough, next morning at the coffee counter a World War II veteran says, "For four years those guys tried to kill me, and now I gotta pay tax money so they can build monuments." Similarly, local politicians were letting voters know that they support appropriations for a convention center or a performing arts center but not for a Japanese cultural center.

Though the Japanese are a significant minority in this county and have extensive property, they are far outnumbered by Hispanic people and Basques. American Indians seem to rank about fourth, close in number to blacks. "The undercount for Hispanic and Basque minorities is high," Dale warns. "There are more ethnic people than the census reports. The official estimate of the undercount runs five to ten percent, but it's more than that." There are others too—a Dutch community, a few Chinese, and some Vietnamese. "But most of them have moved to Portland or Eugene," says Dale. "Can't blame 'em. I would too, rather than be stuck out on some dryland farm nobody can make pay."

The census report indicates that 48 percent of the county's residents live outside incorporated areas, and another 44 percent live in towns of between 2,500 and 10,000 people. I doubt that the majority live in the country and drive to town to work. The few who do that are offset by the town dwellers who drive into the country to farm. So nearly half the population is still involved in agriculture. Increases in tourism will not offset the dominant role of farming in this county for a long time.

The future, however, may show the same dramatic changes here as elsewhere: prison construction will create 300 jobs in one year, and 300 more the next. Though the county is working with the prison on water and sewer issues, no new housing is under construction. Many of the construction jobs, it is hoped, will go to unemployed residents, but the local workforce cannot possibly fill the number of positions to be created in the next ten years. Further, this will be a maximum-security prison—the sentences will be long. The prison administration has said that there won't be an influx of prisoner families, but that doesn't square with any other big prison town's experience. This one will hold 6,000 inmates. Some of their families will surely arrive, but no one is looking at an increase in the number of social workers, who are already overworked here as elsewhere. There is a sense of something pending here, of chickens coming home to roost.

In La Grande I go to the Eastside Tavern for dinner. They have a Baked-Potato Bar Special on Thursday nights: a huge baked potato and a great variety of stuff to put on it. I like this unpretentious place. I have a beer and watch a young woman, apparently of average skill, shoot pool by herself till she has cleared the table and then head to the dining room for the special. On the bulletin board between the bar and the cafe someone has tacked up a family photo and a note. Under a biblical quotation (Psalms 41:1–3, the note says), it reads

> Thank you is such a small expression of how we feel toward all who have given so much of their time, prayers and finances in the fund drive for Bob's bone marrow transplant. . . . We are truly grateful for the part you have played in this urgent struggle for life.
>
> Sincerely,
> Bob, Sybill, and family

In the photo a husky man of about thirty-five with a mustache has one hand on the shoulder of a teen-age son standing next to him and the other on the shoulder of another teen-ager sitting in front of him. To the right is a girl of perhaps ten, and seated in the center is the wife and mother, looking straight and self-possessed into the camera. The note is signed in a feminine hand.

FALLING BEHIND
THE DATA CURVE

This morning I drove across the rolling high plains from Havre, Montana, to Great Falls to attend a meeting with representatives from a number of western Indian tribes and representatives of the state's higher education system. Margaret Kingsland, the director of the Montana Committee for the Humanities, has also come. Her interest in American Indians is widely known and appreciated in Montana, and she is often invited to such events. The purpose of the meeting is to think about how to help Indian students persist in their education from elementary school through tribally controlled community colleges to graduation with a degree from the state university. The new system under consideration will track students from elementary school through the remainder of their academic career, collecting data on their performance all the way. In fact, the project is called TRACKS.

The meeting begins with warm remarks from all sides. The university seems eager to help. The president is very positive about providing information from the college end, letting folks back home know when a student is in difficulty or has left the university. He notes that the difference between drop-outs and stop-outs is important. "In 1990," he says, "less than twenty percent of all college students went through the system in four years. Others stop-out for some time along the way. It's important to keep track of those and to distinguish between them."

Tribal members, in turn, express their appreciation for the educators' interest and for their attendance at this meeting. They are uneasy, however, ambivalent and divided among themselves about the project. Several express reservations about the data collection. Ed Stamper, the delegate from Stone Child Community College, says that confidentiality is a serious issue for his tribes. "Information like that," Doug Sullivan of the Fort Belknap Reservation says, "ought to be collected on everyone, on the white kids too." Joyce Silverthorn, a Flathead, tells us that she has met with parent organizations and a variety of schools. She has found some support for TRACKS but also some fairly strong opposition. She says her people "want to know what kinds of testing will be done. How will we follow up on the information that is gathered?" Some tribal representatives report that their tribal councils are afraid of labeling and that the categories established in collecting the data, all of which have to bear labels, may not fit all tribes. "We're all different," Joyce says. "What works for us may not work for Crow." Tribal concerns about who will see the TRACKS data and how it is to be used become paramount issues, and the meeting almost founders over them. The Indians all know that data collected about them has too often been used against Indians rather than for them.

Perhaps we need to continue to collect data about Indian higher education, but in the case of American Indian schooling, maybe we don't need an additional database. We've been collecting data since the first electronic punched cards arrived on the scene forty years ago. We had some astute observers recording their experience before that, and a number of them since. Robert Havighurst, for instance, conducted a massive study of Indian education published in the early 1970s, and the Northwest Regional Educational Laboratory published an exciting longitudinal study of Indian high school student drop-outs and stop-outs in four Northwest states shortly after. Little changes from one study to the next. We have known for a long time that

Indian students drop out of our educational institutions at an alarming rate, that too few graduate, and that our colleges and universities are alien and inhospitable places for them. Our efforts to prevent Indian high school students from dropping out have ranged from placing them in boarding schools thousands of miles from home to handcuffing them in the basements of those schools. There is already abundant experience to indicate that Native American students are not well served by our educational systems.

It does not take more data to figure out what to do about the problem. What it does take is some experience, a willingness to listen patiently to American Indians telling their stories about schools, and a further willingness to examine that experience and those stories as carefully and honestly as possible. It is essential that we examine not only our minority students and their circumstances but ourselves as well. The task is to examine and reflect on what we already know in our heads and feel in our hearts, and to get back to thinking about our primary experience with real people.

Instead of looking for learning disabilities or learning handicaps in our students, schools from the elementary through the graduate level might look at their own instructional disabilities and teaching handicaps. Indian students learn plenty from their parents and grandparents, their uncles and aunts, and their peers. Our failure to teach them well is our own failure, though we try to blame them. They learn perfectly well outside schools but do poorly within them. We need to examine what we think we know about pedagogy, or perhaps relearn what we've forgotten.

We already know, for example, that we are a racist society. We know that even with the best of intentions (which we don't always have) the institutions we establish reflect the feelings and values of the established culture and as such are inevitably racist or perhaps more accurately culture-based, for none of us can avoid acting out of our own cultural impulses. Our schools are designed, consciously and even more so unconsciously, to enculturate our children. Since they are designed by us, they are not designed to enculturate black children into black culture or American Indian children into tribal culture. Education systems established by the Crows would also be racial (cultural), seeking to serve Crow cultural interests. Crow schools would probably not serve, for example, middle-class Americans from Virginia or American Hmong very well. This would be true especially if classes were conducted in the Crow language, as they should be to serve the culture well, with English taught as a second language. If Crow children or members of another culture are not well served by our institutions, we should not be surprised or doubt for long the stories that American Indian parents tell about their children's difficulties.

The meeting in Great Falls reveals a new vocabulary to conceal our racism. Data collection has become a racist dodge. "We have to establish a baseline before we can do anything," the educators say. "We need more data." The old racist excuses for not doing anything about racist issues were: *They* never apply; *they* don't register to vote; *they're happy* the way they are. Those were, and to some extent remain, our excuses for not hiring, for not encouraging voting, for not changing *our* behavior.

But now we have a new excuse: "We don't know what to do until we identify the problem, and we can't identify the problem until we collect more data," as one non-Indian educator said. This argument only serves our desire to postpone both thought and action. In this view, we don't need to think, because we don't have anything to think about until we have more data. There is no need, apparently, to reflect on our experience or our well-known, well-documented history of failure to provide a meaningful educational experience for American Indian students on our campuses.

But the data-delay syndrome is simply the long, slow curve. When the fast break comes, it has such a hop on it that even the most cynical are surprised. As soon as the argument for data is made and the tribal representatives finally, reluctantly, after long discussion acquiesce to our assertion of its necessity, the educators say, "Well, yes, it's true we do need more data [almost as if data collection were the Indians' idea], but it will take a long time to get it." They then parade a litany of reasons why the data collection cannot proceed. The reasons are familiar: the manpower isn't there; the computer can't handle it; the numbers are not uniform and so are not comparable; the software needed at various sites isn't compatible; there isn't enough money in the budget because we didn't anticipate this project; funds are already committed elsewhere; and on and on.

Collecting data on minorities is always a step toward dehumanization, but in our culture data has become a force that is alienated from its subject, an extraction and an abstraction. It is not the subject, though it tends to become the subject, or to replace it. Depending on our analysis, data may or may not represent the subject. We rarely need (or have an opportunity) to deal with the primary subject because we deal with the data instead. No matter how it is analyzed or used, data remain a secondary or even tertiary level of experience. To form policy or to make plans on the basis of data rather than the subject itself is to do so on the basis of the secondary, the artificial, the surrogate, the unreal, and often the inaccurate or misread. If we rely exclusively on data to chart our course, as many executives, educators, and legislators insist we should, the inevitable results are policies and plans that are without any human or moral foundation, without any evidence of a right mind at work.

Our reliance on data must have T. S. Eliot spinning in his grave. Eliot asked,

> Where is the wisdom we have lost in knowledge?
> Where is the knowledge we have lost in information?

The questions now make him look prescient. There is a real gradation, an intentional value scale explicit in his poem. Wisdom is more than knowledge, knowledge is more than information. Yet now we take pride in living in the Information Age. In Eliot's time, information was among the lesser values; in our time, we have made it preeminent. Why not withhold our self-congratulations until we can say we live in the Age of Wisdom? Such a time will never come, of course, not because we do not have the capacity for wisdom but because wisdom would recognize how little it knows and how trivial information can be.

If Eliot were writing now, I suspect he would add two more categories to the three he mentions, and his disdain would increase as he added each one:

> wisdom
> knowledge
> information
> facts
> data

Data is clearly the low item on this totem pole, yet it has become a huge totem in our culture.

Often we want data not because we need the information it may lead to but because we want the protection it offers if we act. We want to be able to say, "Listen, the data indicated that . . ." and therefore we were justified in our actions. A lack of data offers us an excuse for dragging our feet, and it also induces fear in the average bureaucrat: How can I prove I did the right thing if I don't have the data to show it?

Meanwhile, back at the meeting, fears about confidentiality continue to be a concern among the Indians until a Cheyenne woman reports that her tribe has already begun a tracking system without tribal objections. She thinks the data will transfer easily. But the argument is taken up again by a man from the Fort Peck Reservation who notes that his educators are concerned not only about confidentiality but also about the personnel and the time required to do the tracking. Other tribes react differently. Donovan Archambault, a delegate from Fort

Belknap, says that the idea was well received by the tribal council and school. A tracking system for their community college is already in place, and they have established a team of community members and educators to work on TRACKS. They only need to add the elementary and secondary schools to the system. His report has obvious influence and sways some.

It is no wonder that trust is a serious issue for the tribal councils as they watch us gather more data on their children, and it is no wonder that they feel threatened by the possibility that the data might be misinterpreted or used against them. They are right to see confidentiality as a serious issue. Historically, every time American Indians have revealed themselves to us or allowed the slightest intimacy, they have gotten hurt. They're nuts if they trust us. They have no evidence, not even a byte's worth, to indicate that we are trustworthy. To insist that they participate in a data collection process that will lead to their betrayal is to double the pain. To fail to see, and honor, the reason for their concern about the use to which the data will be put is to ignore history. To argue for more data collection as if it were a means to serve them better is to ignore their experience.

The different attitudes toward the project taken by the various tribes remain unresolved. Nevertheless, as this lengthy meeting concludes, all agree that the new system should stagger on, sidestepping the doubts of the tribes involved and fulfilling the desire of the university for a story it can tell the public about its concern for our first citizens and their higher education.

DESCARTES
ON THE KUSKOKWIM

Isaac is a young Eskimo man who was raised in a Yupik village far out on the Kuskokwim River in southwest Alaska. Isaac is not his real name, of course. Like many other Native people in Alaska, he was given his name by a white missionary who, in his ignorance, could not pronounce the Eskimo name. The power of naming is lodged in our Western tradition in the story of Adam. In Alaska between 1916 and 1970 it was assumed mostly by missionaries and schoolteachers. There is a special irony in Isaac's name; it comes from the Old Testament and means laughter.

Isaac was in Anchorage attending Alaska Methodist University. One night he was drinking in a Fourth Avenue bar and got into a fight. Rather than take him to jail, the police had taken him to the Alaska Native Service Hospital. In those days Alaska Native students at AMU carried an identification card. If they got in trouble with the law or needed some other assistance, they could show the card, which identified them as students and gave my phone number, among several others, as numbers to call.

A policeman had found the card and given it to the doctor who was trying to settle Isaac down. Isaac was "literally ricocheting off the walls," the doctor said when he called to ask if I could take him off their hands. He was "uncooperative and creating havoc, running around, leaping up on desks and counters," and they could not get him to hold still long enough to give him a sedative. When I got to the hospital and walked into the back of the emergency room, Isaac was standing on a gurney like the king of the hill fending off marauders, a huge grin on his face. The doctor and a couple of nurses were standing nearby, watchful but, fortunately, unwilling to use force to subdue him. At the appearance of a familiar face, Isaac yelled, "Cha-mai, Gary!" and jumped down off the gurney. We left without any further trouble.

We sat in my kitchen drinking coffee while Isaac talked. He was still hyper from his experience, still quite drunk, but had been thinking hard about his life and the culture that surrounded him at the university and in the city. Since he talked slowly and with long pauses, not caring a whole lot about what I did, I wrote down as much as I could of what this sobering monologist said as he muttered a critique of our culture that was sobering for me as well. What struck me most was the following not-quite-Cartesian description of his struggle with our culture and his refusal to capitulate to our terms:

> I can't succeed, so I can't prove I exist. You know it, Gary. The white man succeeds at everything. He even thinks he discovered this country. He proves he exists. I can't succeed at anything here, so I can't prove I exist.

> I'm going home. To hell with white man's culture. I've tried to cope with it. I've tried! You know I've tried. I'm going home and live alone—as far from the white man as I can get. To hell with him. Nobody can say I didn't try. I'm going to just fade away. There is no white man's God. There's only shamanism. You know it exists. That's all there is. You know it, Gary, you know it exists. I'm going home and go out on the tundra by myself. To hell with white man's culture.

A GENTILE PILGRIM IN THE PROMISED LAND

The small towns and little junctions of southwest Utah are an anomalous mix of old and new. Modern ranch houses mix right in with older stone or even log buildings. These Utah towns are working towns, but many of them aren't working very well as our century comes to a close. At Todd's (a convenience store and gas stop in Long Valley Junction), over the faucet in the sink in back and next to the ice cream dispenser marked "Out of Order" and the soft-drink dispenser marked "Out of Order" is a sign that says "Unsafe for Drinking." Todd's is run by Dave: long blonde hair, bit of a beer gut but not in bad shape. He looks thirty-eight or so. Actually, he looks like a trucker I knew in Iowa, and he talks like a trucker: "You running again?" he asks a grizzled customer who just came in. "Yeah," the other says, "headed down Flagstaff."

The rural Utah economy has always been tough; now it often seems impossible. The landscape, so cherished by backpackers from Salt Lake and Denver and San Francisco, is beautiful to look at but hard to live on. The neat rows of orchards under the high rimrock at Glendale look productive, but the postmistress, with the perfect timing of Jack Benny, says, "Yes, we grow wonderful apples here . . . when we grow apples. Well, all kinds, I guess, but we haven't had any for about three years now. They blossom and freeze, blossom and freeze, blossom and freeze. We're too small to have a school of our own now. It's down to Orderville, four miles down the road."

The sign on the front of the Glendale store has a letter missing. It reads:"ON_ STOP General Merchandise."The lady who runs this place has another sign up behind the cash register: "Don't steal; the Government hates competition."As far as she is concerned, there isn't much doing in town. Bored, yawning, she says:"We're just waiting for the traffic on the way to the park." She sounded a bit like a woman in another small town far away, Fort Yukon, Alaska. When I asked that woman what she did there, she replied:"Oh, I'm just waiting until the next hanging. Then I'm gonna leave."

I drive on down to Orderville as the postmistress had suggested.Where Highway 89 crosses the east fork of Virgin Creek, three horses stand unmoving in the snow and willows. One is a black-and-white paint, and between the willows and the snow he is almost invisible.When he does appear, he is as ghostly as a horse in one of those ubiquitous Bev Doolittle prints in which horses become trees and rocks mysteriously become sinister faces, conjuring up all the mythology of a West that may or may not have existed.

Orderville fits its name: neat, square, backing away from both sides of the highway, a number of houses being fixed up, little kids on short bikes, faces all screwed up in puzzled wrinkles when they wave to the stranger. It is 3:45 by the time I get there, but school busses are still on the move, so I stop at Valley High School, Kane County School District.

With school over and the buses safely on their way, the principal, Mr. Glover, graciously takes time to talk. The school has 137 students and 11 faculty, he tells me, and the biggest industry in the county is lumbering. "Several of our folks drive truck and such for them."The school building here is only seven years old, "but we weren't thinking when it got built," Mr. Glover reports,"so we have one less classroom in this new building than in the old one we left. We need a new gym and at least one new classroom. Else we're going to have to fix up the old gym for dances and classes and replace the subfloor where the joists are rotting out 'cause the roof leaks."

Orderville has a very low teacher turnover rate, "only two or three in the last three years," Mr. Glover says. Orderville is a "very conservative community, so it is hard for singles here. There's no social life," so single teachers account for what turnover there is. Some, "like the English teacher, come here single, then marry a local boy and stay. She's stayed twenty-seven years. I did that too—met a local girl and stayed." There is another turnover, too, one that is common to small towns everywhere and one that everyone deplores but accepts with a certain fatalism: "All the young people have to leave to find work. There's nothing here for them."

Environmental issues are important, though mention of this sets Mr. Glover to brooding about what environmental protection means in this small place: "Environmentalists have kept out coal here, so people who are holding coal leases won't ever realize that potential. There's a new EIS [Environmental Impact Statement] now that may stop the timber, but I hardly pay attention to 'em anymore. It does look like coal is going to go, over west there. They'll be mining underground instead of strip, so the environmentalists don't object. But it means a heavy truck coming out of there every four minutes twenty-four hours a day, clogging the highway, and that can't be good for us who depend on tourists."

Back on the road I pass flocks of crows in a stubble field, like black chunks of stoker coal scattered in the yellow haze above the snow.

Escalante was originally settled by Mormon farmers, who called it Potato Valley. The current name comes from the Escalante River and is said here with a flat second *a,* as in "Escalandt." The river was named by John Wesley Powell in honor of a Spanish missionary who came close to this area in his own meanderings in the 1770s and far as anyone knows was the first Anglo to travel in Utah.

The public library is closed, so I circle the high school, but every door is locked there too. Crossing the street to the community center, I feel exposed and obvious in the broad High Noon sunlight. I'm the only person in sight anywhere in town, and I think I know how a Mormon missionary must feel in an African village, except I have no partner. An absurd self-consciousness makes me think curtains move, eyes I cannot see peer, that everyone knows I am here and that I am a stranger.

The community center is also locked. The senior center next door is dark but open. I go in, find no one, then hear the sound of voices and make my way downstairs. Three women are visiting—two cooks getting chicken and dumplings ready for dinner and the director of the center, Fay Alvey. We talk, which causes the cooks to get up to cook, perhaps to get away from all the palaver.

I ask Mrs. Alvey about her programs for senior citizens. She's not too excited about the subject: "Programs! I'll tell you, it's sorry to say, but people here want a lot of entertainment but not anything that makes 'em think or lasts too long. There's three or four of those older women who get resentful if a program lasts long enough to interfere with their TV shows. We're *trying* to wake 'em up, but they don't like to."

I mention a project sponsored by the Utah Endowment for the Humanities called Creative Aging. "Aging!" Fay says. "We're doing that all the time, and without any help, either! Maybe the creative part would be good for us." Fay reports that there are lots of older people in this town of less than 500. "The kids all go elsewhere." How many of the elders come to dinner at the senior center? "Depends on the menu. Nights like tonight when we have chicken and trimmings, we'll have a pretty good turnout."

The sawmill is the biggest employer in town, according to Fay. "If it weren't for them, we'd be all shut down. Challenger has a few folks here now. They're a group that takes juvenile delinquents up the canyon to straighten them out. They're using the old school across the street for offices and classes. There's a new school on out the road a way. There used to be agriculture, but since BLM, Forest Service, and the Taylor Grazing all cut back on permits around here, it just drove the sheep ranchers out of business, and most of the cattle raisers too." When I ask about local history, Fay says, "We had a history once, years ago, but it's out of print for a couple of years. The DUP [Daughters of Utah Pioneers] did that one." Fay also mentions that she has written a local history. "Just follow me on home and I'll give you one."

I follow Fay to a house a few blocks away, where I help deliver some quilting frames. We visit a bit with her friend, who is going to start a quilt, then drive over to Fay's modest frame house. There are corrals in the back and to the side, and a few sheds with a windbreak wall to the north. A quilt frame is already up and covered, almost filling the living room.

"That's just tying, not a quilt," says Fay. "It lasts a lot longer than a quilt. I've made hundreds, some for my kids, and for their kids, other relatives."

I enthuse, "They are so beautiful! Your kids'll keep those forever; they'll be heirlooms!"

"They'll sure outlast me," says Fay. She hands me a little brochure. She is modest about her historical accomplishment and says it might be good to think about another one: "The old one had mistakes, but they all do, since they're done by human beings."

The drive from Escalante to Boulder, Utah, twists down through slickrock into Calf Creek Canyon and then climbs, twisting up to a sharp hogback. To the east one looks down into a flash of green meadow and a few ranch buildings. The other side slides off abruptly, the slickrock Navajo sandstone a beige and white chaos descending into the creek. Thin stands of willow and cactus provide a little green on its immediate edges.

Boulder is a town of about 120 residents. It has a two-room school, one teacher, a motel (closed just now), and a drive-in. The principal attraction aside from scenery is Anasazi State Park and Museum.

This western landscape is seen by many who live elsewhere as the most desirable region to create a life, yet it is also one of the most difficult in which to make a living from the land. We have known this since the days of the homesteader. Our western land is at once economical and extravagant, spare and generous, penurious and prodigal. It promises much but welshes on nearly every promise. It is benign in the short term but can be vicious over the long haul. A couple of mild winters and you begin to relax. The next winter kills your children in a blizzard that also, incidentally, takes your livestock. In spring the little rivers rage with snowmelt, the seemingly endless runoff pouring out from the high meadows where it gathers from snow packed in the crevices of still higher peaks. Yet by August the crops are brown and lifeless with drought. For years rural people in the West lived a kind of subsistence life, dependent upon whatever fish and game the land provided, as well as crops, cattle, or small businesses. But the game that bounds garishly from the cover of *Outdoor Life* and *Field and Stream* has always been spotty. Some years all the hills seem to hold are tracks, and tracks, my old hunting partner says, make thin soup.

Today Judi Davis is in charge at the state park museum. This is an Anasazi-Fremont contact area. The Anasazis moved up here from northern Arizona around A.D. 1050 and remained here for 150 years. The main Fremont location was along the Fremont River up near Richfield. This park is the oldest state park in the district. It was not designed with an expectation of any increase in tourists, "So we don't even have a place to sit down," Judi says. "We get kind of jealous of Blanding, places like that, that seem to have so much going on. Yes, apples do well up here too. We've had three or four years of drought, but we have a press, and in the fall we all go down to Allen's place. Last year we pressed two hundred gallons of juice. It's a nice community activity."

Judi's husband is "really the ranger, but he's off to ranger school today, and I'm just sort of filling in. . . . We've been here twenty years." She worries that folks in Boulder are stagnating. "The ballet came once, and everybody turned out, and it was a lot of fun." Judi thought it would be possible to use the school for a community program. "It has the best space, although the ballet was in the church. It would be nice to have something to look forward to," she says wistfully.

I take a tour of the museum, walk the grounds, examine the ruins, and try to get the lay of the land. Then I buy some Anasazi beans at the museum gift shop and cross the highway to get some coffee, which I drink sitting in the sun beside the drive-in.

A citizens meeting is posted in the drive-in's window, so I ask the woman behind the glass what it's about. She tells me it's for local ranchers to organize a protest against the environmentalists who are pushing for the reduction or elimination of grazing permits on BLM land (grazing on what, I wonder). The woman at the window of the little drive-in leaves no doubt about whose side she is on, and she is not out to save the grass.

The struggle of many ranchers now is somehow to justify their lives in the face of the environmental slings and arrows that outrageous fortune is throwing their way. Many are great believers in a herding tradition that they see going way back before there ever was an America at all, or even an Old Testament—a tradition they also view as a proud, even noble one. To be told now that herding was never a healthy life for the environment leaves many angry and many more bewildered. Ranching has no doubt been hard on the landscape, not only here but all over the West. In terms of feeding the world, grain may do it better and more productively, but it would also put many, many more acres under the plow. And how is a person to change now, in midlife, not knowing anything else? Drummond Hadley, a rancher, poet, and essayist down in New Mexico tells me he has been working day and night for weeks already this summer to get water to his cows, losing a few in the process.

At 9,000 feet the summer that already grips Escalante has not yet arrived on Boulder Mountain. The trees are just beginning to leaf out at this level. Only a couple of hundred feet above me there is not a sign of a bud. The late afternoon slant of the sun flares off the rimrock and snow atop the Manti La Sals far to the east, etched in this clear air. But the sunslant skips over the canyons below this pass, leaving them in shadows of varying degrees of blue or purple. This vista, in the nineteenth century, with its precise vocabulary for such things, would have been called sublime.

On a bright Sunday afternoon I head south from Salt Lake City, down Highway 89 through Levan. The city park here is serene, cool, with the trees all leafed out, spring having done its work and summer just moving in to take over. Shadows and sunlight dapple the green grass. At the junction the late afternoon light slams off the white side of an abandoned house, transforming it into a painting by some rural Edward Hopper. South of town, two crows are stalking stiff-legged around a green field. They are so black that sunlight ricochets off their breasts.

Each Utah town has its own distinct character, which is remarkable since the layout is the same for all, dictated by Brigham Young himself. Everywhere the streets are laid out from a central square. At the perimeter lie First South, First East, First West, and First North, followed by Second South, Second East, and so on. The architecture also shares common characteristics in the use of stone or brick and in the layout of outbuildings in the farming communities. The distinctions come from the varied workmanship, the arrangement of new buildings, the animals grazing or the variety of farming undertaken at the edge of town, or the wildlife revealed at dusk. As I drive through, each one offers a view of the possible lives here.

Lilacs are out in Salina. At the four-way stop Mom's Cafe is open, a great old stone building with an ugly concrete facade. Despite the failure of the effort to appear more modern, Mom's still looks less anachronistic and placeless than the contemporary Wasatch Cafe or the Hunger Hut on the strip out on Highway 50—buildings designed to be built anywhere, so they don't fit anywhere. The biggest, most modern business building in town—closed this Sabbath afternoon—is Burns Saddlery. In the cafe a waitress asks two men at a table near the window, "You brothers?" "That's right," says one. "We wasn't gonna be," says the other, "but we had the same mother."

These Utah towns are *working* towns. Everyone has to work to piece together a life that is viable and that provides a few amenities. Many such communities still show signs of their original intentions, which were survival and self-sufficiency. The pens, corrals, sheds, and barns are right next to the old houses, the wood all weathered to a silver gray. These are intentional communities, clearly conceived on a New Testament model of caring for one another. The idea here, judging from these old buildings, was to be as independent as possible, to do as well as one could for oneself so as not to be a burden on others, but it was more complicated than that. Since everyone also belonged to the community, one hoped to prosper so that when hardship struck, one had something to share with those who weren't making it. Beyond that, on the spiritual level in this kind of community the twenty-first chapter of Romans is the model: "When one rejoices, all rejoice; when one suffers, all suffer."

"70 East," the sign says, "Next services 107 miles." I go west to Richfield, only fifteen miles away and proud to announce both a McDonald's and a Best Western on the same billboard. To the east of this valley lies a long spine of severely eroded gray sandstone, a little Hell's Half-Acre covered only partly by sage, the rest by desert pavement. The irrigated valley floor is green except for one unplanted square of about eighty acres without a growing thing on it, a red blanket spread out for a picnic of giants.

My van is low on gas, but no stations are open in the sleepy towns in the canyon east of Ogden. The gauge registers so far below empty that I know there is not enough gas to make even the forty-five-mile stretch to Evanston, Wyoming, so I head toward an ALL-NIGHT CAFE sign winking at the world from a mile off the interstate. There is a gas pump, but the waitress says she can't pump till 8:00 A.M. It is now 5:30, but she says, "There is a place back about six miles that opens at 7:00." I order breakfast, get a book from the car, drink coffee, and read. The waitress wants to talk.

She is about fifty and has been working here for twenty years. She and her husband own the place. He is hard and hits her, and she would like to get a divorce, has stayed in the marriage too long already. She would leave, she says, but fears his ability to take everything and to punish her. "I've worked hard, harder than he has, to make this place into something. I can't lose it all, and he would sure get it all if he thought I was going to quit. Should have done it a long time ago, but I'm scared, you know?"

A trucker, standing at the cash register, has been listening. "Yeah," he says, "you should even now. It never gets better, it only gets worse. Best thing I ever did. I waited too long too, but now I got a wife keeps me on the straight and narrow and liking it."

This morning Springdale bathes in a bright sun. It is mid-March and already warm among these deep southern Utah canyons. I'm here to visit with arts council volunteers, to see what they are trying to do in this small place at the entrance to Zion National Park. I don't have any names to start with here, but it shouldn't be too hard to locate people in this small town. I begin by stopping in at the Pioneer Cafe on Main Street. The waitress who brings my coffee has lived here seventeen years and thinks maybe they have an arts council in town but isn't sure. I call the Chamber of Commerce, but there is no answer, so I stop at a gallery owned by a potter. The shop is closed. I walk around back to an open door and a potter who is busy and doesn't want to visit, but he does say, "Look up Larry McKown at Flanigan's, up the street a ways, on the left."

On my way, I stop at the post office to visit with the postmistress. She allows that "Yes, there is an arts council here, and an active one too." She recommends that I look up Lynn Berryhill, who is the chair, and "one of the active ones." She tells me how to locate Lynn and I say thanks and head for the door. Just as the door closes behind me, the postmistress raises her voice: "By the way, Lynn isn't in town today. She's off at a workshop up in Salt Lake. Be up there through the weekend." I thank her again and go on up to Flanigan's, which turns out to be a motel and restaurant not yet open for the season. New carpet is being laid, furniture stacked up everywhere, folks looking a little frazzled. I find Larry McKown in the back of the restaurant.

"Springdale does have an active arts council," Larry says. "They've done mostly music, but for a couple of years we've had a rep theater group come down, do some teaching, some performances. And last week we had David Lee, the poet from Cedar City, over. And can you tell me what the hell is the difference between the arts and the humanities anyhow? It all seems like it meshes and belongs more together to me." He is enthusiastic, interested, quick but urges me to come back when Lynn is in town. "Perhaps the end of April. That's the last good time, since the tourist season consumes everyone's efforts after that." I agree to that and head the van up through Zion National Park, up into the snow, through the great tunnel, and then back down into the sun, to Kanab.

Kanab is flat, laid out in the traditional pattern of Utah communities of every size. I stop in the public library and visit with Marilyn Watson, the head librarian. She is regionally famous for, among other things, an outdoor book fair that she hosts every summer. She has muscular dystrophy. Her body is twisted, head propped back at about a sixty-degree angle and canted to one side. She is still able to walk, dragging one leg and then the other. She has been the Kanab librarian for ten years, which says something fine about Kanab as well as about her, and her husband. I mention the rave reviews I'd gotten about her Books in the Park project. I have to listen carefully to make out what she says. It helps to anticipate the drift of the conversation and ask questions she can answer with yes or no, but I try to be careful at the same time not to put words into her mouth, let her say what she wants. She wants to know where I'm from. When she finds out it's Alaska, she lights up and tells me about visiting her brother there when he was in the army. "He took me all over!" she exclaims, eyes gleaming at the memory. "So you got down on the Kenai." "Oh, yes," she says, excruciatingly slowly, "it's so beautiful." "And you got to Fairbanks?" "There too. All over."

We have mutual friends in Salt Lake, where I'm headed. Brian Crockett and Helen Cox run a nonprofit organization called the Book Group. They have provided funds, study guides, and even books for Marilyn's summer program, which takes library books out to the city park so that residents can have easy and pleasant access to them. She also provides books and a discussion leader who visits with her constituents about books on a special reading list that Marilyn and the Book Group have agreed upon. Her assistant, Ann, fills out the proposals for such projects, and together she and Marilyn make a team.

"Anything I should tell Brian and Helen?" I ask. "Any messages I can deliver for you?"

"Thanks," she stammers, tongue twisting.

"I'll do it," I say and retreat—inspired, depressed, and elevated all at the same time.

My schedule is a wreck. I don't get back to Springdale until the first week of May, but then Lynn Berryhill is in town, and we have an early breakfast. She is a watercolor painter. When I ask what she paints, she says, "landscapes, still-lifes, or . . ." she points to a beautiful landscape, a poster for an exhibit at a prestigious gallery in Tucson and says that is hers. While I sop up the ignorance I've spilled all over the table like a glass of ice water, I ask Lynn what folks here worry about when they aren't worrying about making a living. She thinks a bit and says, "The same things other folks do, I guess, . . . the environment, politics." I ask if folks here know what they want their town to look like twenty years from now, if they have decided what they want to be when they grow up. Lynn responds with a vigorous shake of her head. "No, that's a real serious problem for us."

As Lynn describes it, Springdale is like a lot of little western towns: divided. To put it in the extreme, about half the citizens here are sure that forty-story condos built up against these beautiful slickrock canyon walls would be wonderful. The other half believe that a teepee by the Virgin River, which rolls through town, would be a tragic intrusion. Both groups think they know and desire the public good. They have yelled across at each other at public hearings so often that they now carry a subliminal, occasionally overt, anger about with them. They long ago quit listening to one another. As in many small communities, there is no escape from the tensions raised by civic strife. If you feel betrayed at the town council on Monday night, the betrayer is apt to be sitting at the next booth in the coffee shop on Tuesday morning.

I ask Lynn if she has read Dan Kemmis's book, *Community and the Politics of Place,* and we talk about Kemmis and others who might have a way of talking about such issues so that Springdale folks could have a neutral setting in which to listen to each other, hear some new ideas, begin to think together about issues in such a way that they can also *live* together without anger. She mentions *Habits of the Heart,* by Robert Bellah, Richard Madsen, William M. Sullivan, Ann Swidler, and Steven M. Tipton. Their book is essential for anyone interested in learning about the state of community in America. We talk about Tom Lyon at Utah State University, who may know more about western American literature than anyone else in the country; Barry Lopez from Finn Rock, Oregon; Bill Kittredge at the University of Montana; Annick Smith, a filmmaker and fiction writer; Mary Blew, author of two wonderful memoirs about growing up in the West; Colleen Cabot, former director of the Teton Science School; Gary Nabhan, cofounder of Native Seeds/ SEARCH in Tucson; and Gary Snyder, a Pulitzer Prize poet and environmentalist in California. Terry Tempest Williams is practically a local, having vacationed in Springdale for many years. All have good ways of talking about the West. Lyon's talk about western writing and his idea of a frontier mind and a postfrontier mind fit this place very well. Kittredge talks convincingly like a "good ole boy" because he grew up ranching, but he now insists that things have to change. We discuss holding a series of meetings that would bring some of these people to Springdale in a format that would make all sides comfortable.

I spend the afternoon on the phone, talking with folks whose names had come up in our conversation, checking to see if they would be willing to come to Springdale. Everyone says yes, it is just a matter of scheduling. The idea seems worth exploring. I also call folks about an evening meeting and talk with others who might like to know what is going on.

Lynn and I meet that evening over dinner with Robert and Naomi Weyher, a retired contractor and his wife, both in their seventies. Louise Excell, a professor of English at Dixie College in St. George, where she commutes each day, is present. Larry McKown had planned to come but became so engaged at the motel that he couldn't, his estimate of schedules after April being dead accurate. When I repeat the questions I'd asked Lynn in the morning, the responses are very similar, the issues the same. Everyone at the table thinks the project Lynn proposed is worth pursuing. Louise and Lynn volunteer to work on a proposal to the Utah Humanities Council for some travel funds so that a series of speakers can come. Everyone thinks the phrase *public good* ought to appear in the title of this series, for that seems to be a virtue that is missing in their town. They also agree among themselves that they need to think hard about the conceptual framework, as well as about a title for this effort. They set out chores that need to be done: arrangements for in-kind housing, meals for our guests, space for the meetings, and talks with other folks in town about the possibilities.

After the meeting I throw all my junk together, pack the van, and check out since there will be no one on the desk at 5:00 A.M. when I have to leave.

"You made thirty-four phone calls today?" says the woman on the desk, astonished.

"Sounds right," I say.

"Jeez," she says, "no wonder your ear looks like that!"

Two weeks later I'm back in Springdale. Louise and Lynn have been talking to people all over town, enlisting their support for this project. Louise has also talked with Doug Alder, the president of Dixie College, and to faculty colleagues on the campus. One of her faculty friends is a former student of Tom Lyon's, and he is especially excited about the prospect of having Tom down in the area. Lynn had a heartening visit with Jamie Gentry, the executive director of the Zion Natural History Association. He's willing to co-sponsor the programs and will let us use park space for some of the meetings. Louise has been thinking about some language for the proposal. They have found a title that fits the concept they are working on—Embracing Opposites: In Search of the Public Good. We agree to stay in touch via phone until they have a solid draft of a proposal in hand.

It is March again. A whole year has passed since my first visit to Springdale. Louise's proposal has been approved by the Utah Humanities Council, and the local arts council has received the funds to bring the speakers to town. I have been invited to attend the opening session, and I begin a celebratory day of driving, happy to be back in Utah again. It is 667 miles from my home in Boulder, Colorado, to Springdale, Utah. Estimated time is twelve hours, and that turns out just about right, allowing plenty of time for coffee. A day of driving in and out of squalls, snow, and rain alternating with bright splashes of sunlight.

In Springdale I have supper with Louise Excell, the project director; Lynn Berryhill, her assistant; and Delmont Oswald, the executive director of the Utah Humanities Council, who has been invited down to share the excitement. Louise reports that the mayor of Springdale has been worried that there is a hidden agenda to this program and will not attend. Delmont agrees to meet with him in the morning. I agree to meet Louise and Lynn to help clean up the Tanner Center, where the evening meeting will take place. They feel sure that there has been good publicity, and their posters and program brochure are indeed handsome and can be seen in every shop and display area in town. Louise and Lynn are happy, excited, and apprehensive. They have such high hopes—and no experience to indicate how things will go. They say they will be disappointed if "only fifty people show up for the evening program" in this little town of perhaps 700 permanent residents. On the other hand, they wonder what to do about the afternoon meeting, which has been designed to be small and intimate. They fear there will be too many people to seat at the tables they have set up.

Next day, at the Tanner Center, we move the furniture, vacuum, set up chairs. Lynn has brought several big bouquets of flowers, and under our spur-of-the-moment pressure she agrees to bring a couple of her paintings to hang on one rather dreary wall. David Pettit, Louise's husband and a fine photographer, also agrees to bring some of his photographs. The room looks great.

We have almost a hundred chairs set up and extras available if necessary.

After lunch Del and I pick up Dan Kemmis and take him into Zion National Park, where the afternoon roundtable will be held. In addition to the local folks there are representatives from other towns in the region: the mayor of Virgin, for example; a couple of town council members from Toquerville, fifteen miles down the road; and four or five people, including the chief of police, from Aspen, Colorado. There are too many to sit at the table, perhaps forty-five or fifty altogether, including the mayor of Springdale. The moderator introduces everyone, asks a couple of questions, and people begin to talk. The tensions between development and conservation, between the arts community and the necessary commercial enterprises surface quickly and, despite some strain, are discussed frankly and with surprising candor. At the end, everyone is excited and pleased, and interest is high for the evening.

When I arrive at the evening event fifteen minutes early, the place is already swamped. People are setting up extra chairs, and a partition has been pulled back to make extra space. When things settle down, Dan Kemmis begins by describing democracy in Athens. He talks about American democracy and Thomas Jefferson's hopes for it, and then about our current practices in local government and how they fall short of democracy. He talks about the tensions that inevitably arise in small communities, about some of the things that Missoula has tried in an effort to restore democracy, and about the good faith and trust that must develop if we are ever to discover the public good and find ways to act on it.

Kemmis's talk is low-key but intense, everyone listens intently, and there is that good tension in the room, the kind that comes from involvement and inspiration. After Kemmis finishes his formal presentation, questions from the audience go on for over an hour. Even after the question period, people linger to visit, reiterating what Kemmis has said, arguing over this point or that. By the time we clean up, douse the lights, and cross the parking lot, it is 11:30. I congratulate Lynn and Louise and beg off the reception still going on at Bob and Naomi Weyher's home.

The next morning Dan Kemmis, Lynn Berryhill, and David Pettit prepare for a hike in Zion, Louise takes off for work, Delmont Oswald leaves before breakfast to get to another meeting, and I pack for the drive to Boulder, Colorado. This is just the beginning for Springdale. The town has five such meetings scheduled on successive Fridays. Jordan Paul, a psychiatrist from Aspen, is next, followed by Terry Tempest Williams, Bill Kittredge, and Tom Lyon.

Months later the Springdale programs will win an award from the Utah Humanities Council as one of the best programs of the year. They will also win the Schwartz Prize, given by the National Federation of State Humanities Councils for the best public humanities program in the country. The citizens of Springdale have taken a courageous step, bringing difficult conversations about their community, its fragmented divisions, and personal antagonisms into a public arena. It has worked for them. One outcome was a first for the town: a community picnic that brought everyone to a small park and ball field for a potluck celebration. The awards I mentioned are significant, and winning them is appropriate and richly earned, but perhaps the most telling evaluation came from a restaurant dishwasher whom I asked about the picnic. "Oh," he said, "that was great! Everybody came! I saw people there I never saw at anything in this town before."

Over in Richfield the town park is a big square cut up into useful sections by lilac bushes. I stop in the park for supper—whatever is left in the grub box: some cold cereal, milk, a couple of week-old bagels, peanut butter, plastic margarine that never seems to age and won't melt under any conditions, and jam. There are swings in the park, a teeter-totter, and tables in the shade under big cottonwoods. A child is screeching with delight as her mom, quite pregnant, thrills her with bounces on the teeter-totter.

I am in the lee of a row of lilacs about a hundred feet away. They reduce the wind a bit, but it still carries the strong, slightly acrid smell of lilac across to me. I fix the cereal, eat a bagel, reject a second, then decide to eat it, knowing that if I don't I'll throw it away, and that is a sacrilege. In my mind I can see my mother smile at this decision (really made when I was about four years old), so I eat everything in the grub box, in praise of lilacs and wind and children yelling for the sheer pleasure of it and pregnant mothers playing, and remembering the starving Armenians, though I've never understood why my eating too much will benefit those who cannot get enough. It isn't quite bread and wine, but the elements are basic enough, and for this moment, in this place filled with slowly waning light and darkening shadows and children's voices, it is perfect. I try to remember if purple is the color of epiphany, but I think it's green, which is okay too. Or is it white?

A LITTLE WESTERN
ADVICE

On the interstate between Boise, Idaho, and Ontario, Oregon, an early evening deer bolts from a depression in the median strip. I swerve, tearing precariously along a steep shoulder, two wheels in the bar pit, my '89 Caravan ripping up grass and wheat and spewing gravel, then, rear two wheels off in the ditch, slough down along the side of the bar pit like a cat scrabbling not to fall, until finally, trying to resist the impulse to oversteer, I swerve back onto the interstate, the violent rocking reminding me of a fishing boat rolling in a heavy chop.

At the next exit I pull off to survey the damage. The van looks like the Auto from Oz, wisps of yellow straw and grass spraying out at every angle, drooping off the bumper like a mouth dangling spaghetti, a wide fan between grill and hood, grass even trapped under the windshield wipers. Alas, underneath there is a big spray of gasoline from the tank and another leak that seems to be something else—brake fluid or oil, maybe. I can't tell which, but I check the exhaust and muffler especially carefully, making sure there will be no errant sparks when I start up. Despite Robert Frost, I have no desire to go in either fire or ice, or in a bar pit for that matter.

In Ontario everything mechanical is already closed, so I check into a Motel 6 only three blocks from a Dodge garage.

The fuel is low enough in the tank that when I park on a slight incline the gas stops leaking.

At seven o'clock the next morning I am first in line when the garage opens. On the hoist it is easy to see that the gas tank is thoroughly bashed in, both leaks coming from tears at the front. The radiator, engine compartment, and undercarriage are all bristling with dry grass. "We'll clean all that out under there and replace the tank," the man says. "Do it all for about two hundred and fifty dollars, but I have to order a tank from outta town. Take a day or two."

I ask if I could drive it, as I had been, while we wait for the tank to come. "Well," he says slowly, as if pondering, "I sure wouldn't recommend that." Finally, after a long pause, he goes on. "One spark and you'd depart this world," he says, rolling his eyes skyward as if watching my body arc about sixty feet in the air. "We'd never see you again. Then, when the new tank comes, who'd pay for it? . . . Be a terrible thing for us."

GULLS

ON A HIGH WIND

On the first day out in the summer of '65—my first day ever on a fishing vessel—the weather was blowing about twenty-five knots, but it was relatively warm and clear. We ran south and west a while, the Bristol Bay gillnetter lunging and rocking in the chop. Hank yelled, "Drop the pick!" I was green and stupid and didn't know what he meant, wasn't even sure of his words, exactly, through the sounds of the wind and water. It was clear that he couldn't possibly be asking me to go up in the bow and drop that heavy anchor overboard, though it occurred to me that *pick*—if that's what I'd heard—could mean anchor. But the bow was rising and falling at a rate leading to certain death. I could not comprehend, would not comprehend, that he really wanted me to go up there and do that. I could get killed! And the first day out, no less. Hank yelled again, disgusted. It was clear that he meant what I was afraid he meant, so I did it, clinging fearfully to anything that offered a hold. On the bow deck I got down on hands and knees to maintain my balance while lifting the hook. Hank shut the engine down and walked up as if we were ashore, grabbed the anchor, and tossed it—as if it were a mere beach pebble or a chip of bark—twenty feet off in the dark water. From then on I did the walk too, though for a couple more days it was all sham and sheer bravado. I remembered a baseball coach in Iowa when I was a kid yelling at me after I struck out, "If you can't *be* a hitter, at least *look* like a hitter!" Once my corn-shucking legs got the sea lurch mastered, it was a breeze. Before I fished, I would have worked in the bay for nothing, just to have the experience. After that first day, I wouldn't have done it except for a heck of a lot of money, the only reward available except for the satisfaction of having learned to do it well—a satisfaction, given my green sea legs, not to be underestimated.

I commercial-fished for red salmon as a boat-puller on the *Lori—K.O.,* a Bristol Bay gillnetter, for two summers while teaching school in Naknek, Alaska. Hank Ostrosky was the skipper. Most of the year he was an electrical engineer, working at the White Alice site in King Salmon, eighteen miles down the only road in the region, linking Naknek to the air station there. He took off work from June 20 until July 20 each year to commercial fish the red salmon runs up the Naknek and the Kvichak Rivers of Bristol Bay, in the Bering Sea just north of the Alaska Peninsula, which extends for hundreds of miles out into the Pacific, ending in the Aleutian Islands. The bay was home to other red salmon runs as well, the Egegik and Nushagak, for instance, but Hank had fished the Naknek district for many seasons.

Though we haven't fished together for thirty years, we have maintained a connection, one so solid that it may be impossible to break no matter how much we may offend one another in the very different lives we lead now. Since I have moved back to the Lower 48, the connections are maintained by occasional telephone calls and by memories. The latter are far more important, crucial even, to the relationship, perhaps because the bonds were forged in the kinds of events that reshape lives. All it takes is a high wind for Bristol Bay and the many faces I knew and things I learned there to come back to me, always with Hank at the center. In fact it was a phone call, with Hank's voice on the other end of the line, that bound us together in the first place. The memory of that call still holds me.

The bay and Hank came back to mind when my wife, Lauren, and I were holed up in a small cabin right over the ocean on the Oregon coast. We were surrounded by trees, miraculously clear skies, and the sound of waves and birds. The last day of our stay began clear, the ocean flat-calm, the waves just curling inshore. But the gulls were drifting as high as or higher than the trees on our high sea cliff—a sure sign, an Eskimo student once explained to me, that the wind will blow. Ever since, when the wind blows I find myself watching the birds, even far inland, and earth and the weather become the trigger of memory. By noon a breeze had come up, and by 2:30 there was a pretty fierce chop, whitecaps hacking the surface of the blue water. All the boats that had been playing or working off the shore were gone, apparently heeding the small-craft warnings that had been posted as the wind came in from the north-northwest at twenty-five to thirty-five knots.

Wind blowing at twenty-five knots from out of the southwest was the kind of day fishermen in Bristol Bay used to think was perfect for fishing. "The wind blows the fish up the bay," they'd say. Everyone would be out, two men to a boat, the little thirty-two-foot drift boats rolling from side to side, riding up the waves and rocking violently in the inevitable Bristol Bay chop. In a real blow a wave would sometimes curl out from under the keel and the bow would fall so fast your feet would leave the deck. At the bottom of the trough the boat would smack into the water so hard that your knees would buckle. Twenty hours of that was enough to make you appreciate a soft bed and make you think you'd earned your pay. Five days of a steady blow was enough to give you the blind staggers, make you walk, onshore, like Uncle Harry late on Saturday night.

Hank put great store in science and technology, believed that the answers to every question would ultimately be solved by science, and was a devoted and comprehending reader of *Scientific American* and the *Bulletin of the Atomic Scientists*. Since I was far more skeptical about the efficacy of both science and technology, we argued, vehemently, occasionally at the top of our lungs—long, outraged conversations about the blindness and stupidity of the other. Hank swore he was an atheist; I accused him of making a religion of science and worshipping at the altar of technology. He said that I had a nineteenth-century brain, that if a machine did not run on kerosene, I couldn't make it work. We were both right.

Together with Hank's wife, Katherine, we put out a home-made newspaper, the *Bristol Bay News,* using a mimeograph and a scanner Hank had in the cellar. The latter made a pretty fair screen so that we could reproduce photos. Hank wrote the editorials, I typed, and we all stapled, folded, stamped, and addressed. Typing earned me the title of assistant editor. It was surprising how many times Hank got quoted by the two statewide newspapers in Anchorage or had stories picked up by the wire services.

In Naknek, fishing was the great occupation around which every life swirled and circled, swam or sank. Before I went to Naknek, if you had said to me, "Peter Pan," my mind would have gone instantly to James M. Barrie, Mary Martin, a green figure sliding across the stage on a wire, the English theater. In Naknek my schoolkids, indeed everyone, would have thought of a cannery by that name just down the beach from the village. To me, *cow* conjured up images of holsteins on a hillside, milk, green midwestern pastures, and red barns. Bristol Bay kids called a fat red salmon ready to spawn a cow, and they knew about milk—that it was a white powder, came in a large red-and-white cardboard box, and had to be mixed with water. It was called Carnation. Neither cows nor milk had any connection with real carnations or a four-legged creature. It was apparent that I had a lot of learning to do and that I was beginning with an inadequate understanding of English.

Men in the village never talked baseball scores and did not know the names of professional football teams. There was no television as yet. Fish, boats, nets, and sometimes hunting for moose or caribou were the routine talk of the day, supplemented by conversations about the Japanese interception of Bristol Bay salmon stocks on the high seas and the uninformed, uncaring indifference of the U.S. State Department to the international high seas robbery of American fish from our nets. "The U.S. government cares more about the Japanese than it does about us" was a complaint transformed by repetition to the status of cliché. Considering the high stakes involved in our relations with Japan compared to the poor incomes of a few thousand fishermen, the contention seemed plausible.

There were 2,400 boats in the bay and not enough fish. Fishermen would "cork off" each other, or snarl another's gear. Along with stopping the Japanese on the high seas, we all said, we had to limit the number of boats. We concluded that the way to do that was to thin out the fishermen for whom the bay meant a second income: the teachers and missionaries and doctors and dentists from Anchorage or Fairbanks.

Naknek itself was a subarctic version of the classic company town in the northwest logging country or the Appalachian coal mining region. Groceries came from a company store, and boats were leased or bought on time from the cannery, to which each fisherman owed his catch and his allegiance. At the end of the season, after the year's groceries and the boat payments were deducted, little was left for the winter.

The bay was famous throughout Alaska as the most difficult and dangerous fishery on the coast. There were other places of great danger: fishing the surf out of Yakutat or crabbing in the winter on the open North Pacific out of Kodiak or Dutch Harbor. At times these are even more dangerous than the bay, but of the summer fisheries, Bristol Bay was known for continuous bad weather exacerbated by fierce storms and complicated by the fact that, except for the ship channel in the center, the bay was shallow. The ocean here does not roll in long, even swells; it has a madhouse chop that seems to come from every direction.

Because its fishery was one of the earliest and largest in Alaska, the bay had an aura akin to legend, not only among other fishermen in the state but in other American fisheries as well, and far beyond. Once Alan Villiers, the famous English seaman who sailed a replica of the Mayflower to America, gave a talk in Anchorage. I was in town and went to hear him. Later that night I ran into him on the elevator and told him I'd enjoyed the talk. "You sail?" he asked. "No," I replied, "closest I've ever come is fishing in Bristol Bay." "Oh," he said, shaking his head, eyes flaring with knowledge. "That's no good, no damn good. Too rough, too damn rough."

For years the bay was fished with small, wooden double-enders, whose bow and stern were shaped the same. They were equipped with a single mast and sail. Powerboats were outlawed in the bay until 1954. Until then, fishermen would be towed or would row out to the fishing grounds, hoist a sail, sleep (if sleep was possible) in a canvas pup tent rigged in the bow, and cook on a single-burner "Swede stove" fueled with gas. The weather is so bad in the shallow bay, and the sea so fierce, that one can hardly imagine the work. Each year the bay claimed lives, sometimes twenty or thirty in a single season.

Local Alaska Natives were excluded by law from the fishery for many years, and many of the fishermen were brought up from San Francisco on the old four-masted sailing schooners that worked the trade. They would leave San Francisco loaded with all the supplies necessary to can fish: tools, tin for the cans, food for the crews for the summer, and bedding for the bunk-houses. Sometimes they would leave San Francisco too early in the spring or depart Naknek too late in the fall, the weather would turn cold, and the ships would freeze in the ice. I have seen flickering old movies of those ghostly ships, frozen into the North Pacific, the men walking around like they were ashore, peering up at the ship as if it were in dry dock. Most were Scandinavians or Italians. Their lives were hard and from a distance, perhaps, romantic. They used to say, "We pulla the boat to catcha the fish to getta the mon to buya the bread to getta the strength to pulla the boat." "He's my boat puller," Hank would say, introducing me and putting me in my proper historical context.

When I worked in the bay, the boats were stored in a warehouse on the dock through the winter and dropped into the water again by a crane in the middle of June. There were several kinds: large skiffs, Cook Inlet rigs with a power reel amidship that let out the net and hauled it in, and Bristol Bay boats that laid out net either by hand or over a hydraulic roller. These latter came in two varieties: bow pickers and stern pickers, named according to the area of the boat where the net was laid out and hauled in. If the fishermen were lucky, the net would come in with a real load of fish, called a jag, tangled in the mesh.

The first couple of weeks were spent "scratching" for fish, catching a hundred or two a day. The big run came through over a three- to five-day period, that peaked around July 4 and then quickly tapered off. The competition was fierce, the season short. If you missed the fish during any open period, you might well have missed the season. Often the season was over, and fishermen were back to scratching again, by July 10.

That summer of '65 the bay was alive with a record run of fish. Since salmon swim near the surface, their fins were visible everywhere. There were so many that sometimes only a single fifty-foot shackle of net could be let out at a time, instead of the usual three. It would fill so fast with so many fish that a longer net would sink and be impossible to haul over the roller into the boat. Once, over on the west side of the bay near King Salmon Creek, we let out a shackle and hit the water a couple of times with a boat hook, driving the fish into the net in a furious tumult of thrashing water and salmon struggling not to drown. We had to haul in immediately to keep the net from sinking. Near the mouths of little feeder streams draining into the bay there were so many fish in the water that the prop would hit them. It felt a bit like driving on a gravel road, with the prop going tunk, tunk, tunk, tunk as it cut a path through the salmon.

The radio was always on. We listened for weather but mostly to hear fishermen in other places letting their partners know where the fish were running: "They're really smoking over here on the west side," or, "Come on up to Graveyard. There's jumpers and I'm laying out now." One evening two Eskimo men began to talk, just visiting. One called to the other in English, "Bear, this is the Walrus," but as soon as the Bear replied, they both switched to Yupik. The Yupik language is among the most mellifluous in the world. Unlike our staccato English of single-syllable words inherited from our Angle and Saxon ancestors, the Eskimo languages use stems and suffixes to put together a whole sentence in a single word. The soft voices of the men went back and forth quietly and musically while the *Lori—K.O.* rocked in an easy sea, water lapping along the hull near my head as I lay in the bunk. When the conversation was over, their voices rose and hardened as they switched abruptly back to English: "Okaayeee, this is the Walrus out. Good night."

The allowable catch was determined by escapement, the number of fish available to go on up the Naknek or the Kvichak to spawn. When enough fish had gone up the rivers, the surplus was available to the fleet. Announcements were made via CB radio to let the fishermen know when a period would open and how long it would last. If there were plenty of fish, the period might be extended. Crews would go to their boats, anchored up in the river mouth, and head out into the bay on the high tide just previous to the period's opening. We would guess where the fish might be in the greatest numbers, anchor at the site, and wait for the period to begin.

Frequently when the big run hit, the boats were put on limit, the catch held down to two thousand fish a period. This was because the canneries could not handle the glut if there were more. This was a sad, frustrating, angry time—sad because it was not possible to keep a close count of the catch, and any "overs" had to be dumped back into the bay; frustrating because no one believed that the canneries couldn't gear up to handle the numbers of fish that came with every good run; and angry because in a good season there were plenty of fish, so a fisherman could dream of really getting ahead, paying off the boat, getting out of debt, and saving some for emergencies. Watching the fish go by because you'd hit the limit for your boat, seeing friends weep while pitching their excess fish overboard, knowing it could have been handled better by management—everything combined to create anger and frustration.

One weather report warned of gale-force winds late in the evening. At 1:00 A.M. we were below Johnson Hill, just inside the boundary marker beyond which it was illegal to fish. Johnson Hill is a pile of rock and aggregate that geologists say slid to the east side of the bay from a mountain clear over on the Pacific side of the Alaska Peninsula. At a couple hundred feet elevation, it is the only prominent landmark above the tundra's sandy bluffs on the east side of the bay. We were drifting, Hank and I arguing yet again over his faith in science and scorn for the world's idiot religions, the gillnet strung out behind us with its white corks bobbing in the chop, when the wind began to freshen. It had a feel to it. We watched for a few minutes, the argument already seeming unimportant. The wind came on quickly, sudden driving gusts, and we began to haul in our gear. The nets were full, with a good jag on. Hank began to run for the mouth of the Naknek River, and I stayed in the stern to pick fish, untangling the net from around their gills and throwing them into the hold.

The wind was blowing so hard and the sea running so high that we made little headway. Hank seemed delighted at the challenge of keeping the boat pounding directly into the waves to avoid shearing off and rolling over. "Look at that!" he'd yell every once in a while, as if exhilarated. "Green water right over the bow!" The boat felt like it was hitting a brick wall. It would wallow shakily up one wave and then fall into the trough or slam into the next wave, shaking and shivering "like a dog shitting peach seeds!" Hank would sing. For hours, every time I looked up from picking fish out of the net, with my back to the bow to shed the spray, there was Johnson Hill in the same position on my left.

When we finally got to the mouth of the Naknek, the wind shifted, blasting from the east straight down the river. Instead of being a refuge, the river was as choppy as the bay, and the boats already anchored up were rocking and bobbing. I had hoped we would anchor, but Hank wanted to deliver our catch. Delivery meant pulling alongside a scow and my stepping from our gunwale to a narrow ledge, perhaps a foot wide, along the gunwale of the scow in order to tie up while Hank stood in the cabin fighting the wheel to keep us close. The scow's walkway would be covered with fish gurry, blood, scales, and slime. I did not relish the chore and knew exactly what would happen if I slipped between the two boats.

But Hank found the scow that the Nelbro Cannery had sent out to collect the catch, and pulled alongside. I stepped onto our gunwale, about ten inches wide, balancing with one hand on the cabin roof. The weight and size of the 110-foot scow meant that it reacted to the waves at a different rate than our fiberglass 32-footer. The water would lift us up higher and faster than the scow, and as the scow lumbered up to our level we would fall into a trough, our fenders slamming against the larger boat, and the scow's rail would loom high above my head before it started down as we rose again. It was a wild dance, like mad elevators going in opposite directions and unable to stop at the same floor. When the scow's crew saw us, they came running to wave us off, to my immense relief. We anchored and slept. The wind blew throughout the day—eighty-five knots and gusting higher, we learned. Thirty boats swamped or sank out in the bay. Miraculously, no one drowned.

The next day was flat calm, the bay like glass, as peaceful as it had been violent a few hours before. We had delivered and were back down by Johnson Hill when the radio bleated a Mayday. We listened to see where and if we were needed, but a scow had picked up the signal and was talking to the skipper.

"We're getting a signal," the scow said, "but can't tell where you are. Identify yourself and tell us your ten-twenty."

"This is the *A. Parr,*" the skipper said. "I'm about four miles from the mouth of the Naknek and a little south, and I'm swamping."

"The *Aparr? Aparr?* What the hell is the *Aparr?*" the scow asked.

"The *Fred A. Parr!*" the skipper yelled into his mike, getting frantic. "Fer Christ's sake, you can tell which one we are! We're the only boat in the bay that's going down! The water's up to the cabin and I'm hanging on the antenna! You can *see* which one we are!"

One night we lost our transmission over on the west side of the bay in an area marked Dead Man's Sands on the charts. It was a shallow area where a boat caught on a fast-ebbing tide would go aground. But the shallowness was deceptive. There was no way, despite the acres of sand, to walk ashore. We tried everything to get the transmission to go, but there was no forward, no reverse. Just before it had quit entirely, we had been kicking up sand with the prop, ticking bottom in the shallows and leaving behind a cloudy wake. An Italian bow-picker from San Francisco, seeing we were in trouble, came close and the crew yelled across to see if we could use a tow. Hank yelled "No!" across the wind roar and waves, and the orange hull, low in the water, veered away.

My heart sank. Unless we could fix the transmission immediately, we would go aground. Then there was nothing to do but wait twelve hours till the next tide came blasting in. It would smash our boat to pieces. While Hank revved the engine and threw the transmission into and out of gear, I thought about things. One thing was clear: I did not want to drown on Dead Man's Sands. If only we could get back to the mouth of the Naknek River, I thought, I'd gladly drown over there. It seemed closer to home somehow, while the Sands seemed very far from my world. I also learned something about money. I stood to make pretty high wages because the season had gone well, but if I did not live to collect it, what was the use of money? Further, if I did live, then by God I had the right to spend that money any way I damn well pleased. I'd laid my life on the line for it, and no one could tell me I ought to save it, be frugal, or invest it wisely.

While I mused, Hank gave up. He suddenly raced from the cabin to the bow and began to wave at the Italian boat, already nearly out of sight. But the men aboard knew we were wrong to refuse their tow and were watching us with binoculars. They turned and worked their way back toward us, a tricky proposition since they too had been kicking up sand when they were alongside. Now they somehow managed to get close enough to throw us a line, jerk us to deeper water, and begin the perilous work of leading us home. It is easy to shear off a wave during a tow and turn turtle. A man from South Naknek had done just that, and though he survived, he could not extricate his mother, who died while he clung precariously to the hull throughout a long night's blow before anyone could reach him. We were lucky and were in skillful hands. The Italians towed us across the bay, into the river, and up to the Nelbro dock. Then they flipped us loose and swung back into the river with a wave and a shout.

At the end of the season I flew to Seattle, went directly to a sporting goods store, and bought a forty-dollar Fenwick fishing rod, feeling recklessly, extravagantly self-indulgent and glad to be alive.

The bonds between ourselves and others are forged in different ways. Fishing together as Hank and I did can do that sometimes. You come out of the event like combat buddies, survivors of hellish times. But that did not work for us. We came off the boat eager to be away from each other. Our bonds would have to be forged of harsher, ultimately tougher, stuff.

Hank and Katherine had three children—Lori, Julie Ann, and Zeck. Zeck was the apple of Hank's eye, his only son, a bright-eyed chip off his father's block. After I moved from Naknek to Anchorage, Zeck came into town to spend Thanksgiving. On Saturday I took him over to spend the rest of the weekend with other friends, Guy and Nancy Martin. Nancy put Zeck on the Northern Consolidated flight on Monday morning to return to King Salmon, where Hank would pick him up.

Early that afternoon, Hank called to tell me the plane had not arrived. No one knew yet just what had happened or where the plane was, but we knew it was down because too much time had elapsed. It had to be out of fuel. When he called again, Hank said that a portion of the plane's wing had come off in violent turbulence and the F-27 had crashed with no survivors while making its final approach near Nondalton. Hank was headed to Nondalton to see about Zeck's body. He and Katherine had been talking, he said—voice quavery, then breaking—about a memorial service. Katherine wanted one, insisted on one. Hank had insisted that there would never be one in the local church, though it was the only building that would hold enough people. They had arrived at a compromise: If I would conduct the service so they could avoid having the local clergyman do it, Hank would agree to it.

Our talk had been interrupted by long pauses, and I was shaken not only by Zeck's death but also by the sound of this bluff fisherman, so strong and wholly without fear, gulping down tears, struggling to regain an element of control, making concessions he would never have made except in extreme grief.

Nancy Martin and I flew out to Naknek the next morning. The Northern Consolidated people at the counter looked shocked and vacant, moving mechanically through their tasks, unable to hide their tears. Nancy and I stayed the week with Katherine and the girls while Hank was in Nondalton looking for the parts of Zeck's body that might be identified. The weather remained so foul and cold that it hampered efforts to find bodies and investigate the cause of the crash. It was Friday before they had the body parts gathered up, sorted as best they could, and laid out in the school gym. Hank wanted Zeck buried up near the little lake behind town. John Lundgren and I tried to dig a grave, but the wind was still high, and the temperature was so far below zero that we could not dig in the frozen tundra, underlain by permafrost, and had to give that up.

Everyone in the village came to the service, but it was not the service, nor my intimate involvement with Zeck's death— I had to resist thinking of it as complicity—that finally bound Hank and me in a permanent bight. It was hearing Hank on the phone, his pain exposing him down to the marrow. He was unmanned. Hearing and feeling that raw anguish over the wire was like sharing a secret that only two would know. Grief is rarely secret, of course, and Hank's pain became obvious to others, but it created a kind of intimacy perhaps only grief allows, and it was sacred. Perhaps that is why it lasts.

Since then Hank and I have had our differences, occasions when the arguments have become bruising verbal brawls, and sometimes he'd stomp out of my Anchorage office sounding like he had finally written me off, leaving me depleted and my secretary with her jaw agape. Sometimes we simply let each other down or disappointed each other profoundly. Two or three weeks later he would be back in my office as if nothing had happened.

When the *Challenger* blew up, pieces blasting away from the orange flame to fall through the blue sky, Hank came into the office just as I was watching a replay on our office television. He'd come to tell me that he thought it was a good thing. I was thunderstruck, unbelieving. He persisted, had a whole argument thought out, how it would "get the culture to focus on the important stuff instead of tinkering around in space," how it would "reorient our values." He went on, launching into a real diatribe, while the anger in me built.

I was thinking about Zeck, could see in my mind the wing tip on the F-27 breaking, and remembered Hank on the phone that day years before. The whole world's sadness came down. Finally, unwilling to put up with his talk any longer, I blurted, "Of all people to say deaths like those are a good thing! You should know better. I can't believe it." He argued right back, and I finally said, "I'm not going to listen to this anymore. You can stay here as long as you like, but I'm getting out." I stalked out of my office, leaving Hank slumped, looking a little vague, eyes vacant.

I did not know what a fool I had been until the next day, having coffee with a friend. She knew of my connection to Hank, and I recounted the collision we'd had, my surprise and shock. She said slowly, thoughtfully, "He must have been feeling incredible pain to react that way." I knew instantly that she was right and knew who had let his own feelings get in the way of another's, and it wasn't Hank. But Hank was gone, back someplace in the bush and out of touch. Two months later he was back with a new story about new events, new ways to change the whole universe so that justice would reign supreme at last. No hint that we had ever been estranged, no need to forgive and therefore no need to be forgiven.

We'll go on, I suppose, occasionally abusing each other till one or the other of us dies, my memory of that early phone call washing the slate clean every time, at least for me.

In the afternoon Lauren and I climbed down the sandy Oregon sea cliff, so much like the bluffs over the Naknek where the river spills into Bristol Bay. We took a walk on the beach, a couple of miles down toward the Yaquina lighthouse. At low tide one can get around a point a quarter mile or so down and walk on until the tide and the rocks meet below the lighthouse and prevent further access. Going down, the wind was at our backs, the sand scuttling and flowing ahead of us in little sheets, settling again in pale drifts, drier and lighter colored from its sojourn in the wind than the sand it came to rest on. On our return the wind was a constant roaring in our ears, the sand stinging our faces, the gulls still drifting high.

Next morning we packed up reluctantly, both of us wishing we could stay longer, and drove up the coast to Seattle. We plowed through a heavy sea of traffic all the way, like an old double-ender with a jag on and sail set, indelible images from fishing in Bristol Bay, dormant since the last high wind, still at full flood in my mind.

COHO SMITH

The road south of Soldotna is a white tunnel between black spruce opening into gray sky. A few feet above my windshield a raven drifts precariously on the wind. For a brief distance he is so low and close I worry about hitting him, but he veers off into the spruce, a dark flick of wings lost in the black trees. The roadway is rapidly filling with drifting snow, and winter light turns the whole world—trees, snow, sky, road, and raven—into the tones of an antique photo. The big flakes blow parallel to the earth as if reluctant to settle in an inhospitable landscape.

I'm on my way to the cabin of Coho Smith—Smitty—who lives above the beach on the Kenai Peninsula, south of Anchorage. Some folks, including me, think Smitty's cancer has caught up with him again, but he says that according to the doctors it has been arrested. Yet he admits to pain in his back and continues to lose weight. His complexion is jaundiced, faded far from its normal outdoor ruddiness, and the muscular six-foot frame doesn't move with its customary ease and strength, has become awkward with tiny tics and lurches.

For now, Smitty is living alone. His wife, Mary, occupies another cabin up the beach a few miles. She and Smitty have had a long, tenuous, complicated connection, alternating closeness and intimacy with long periods of separation. Mary is a bird-watcher, and not exactly an amateur. She has recorded sightings of several species not known to be in Alaska and is held in great respect by ornithologists around the country, who correspond with her eagerly. I have no idea what lies behind their relationship and do not care to ask.

Smitty is a commercial fisherman and has lived in Native villages from southeastern Alaska to Barrow. His most recent turn was as a cannery foreman near Unalakleet. We first crossed paths out in Bristol Bay, in Naknek, where I was teaching school.

My first winter in Alaska, Smitty was fishing with the men of the village, using a net under the ice on Naknek Lake, a better trick than it might seem to the uninitiated. A gillnet cannot simply be stuffed through a hole in the ice; it has to stretch out to its full length and be anchored so it will hang suspended in the water. Smitty had invented a creeper, a device that crawled along under the ice, dragging the net behind. Smitty had cammed the creeper so that it bumped against the ice as it traveled. Those above could follow the sound. When it tapped the ice at its furthest extension, the fisherman cut a hole and anchored the net. The hole was enlarged later so that the net, filled with fish, could be pulled up. That was a lean time for the village following a disastrously poor red salmon run, and the lake fish were all brought back to the community hall and distributed to any family short of food. The government shipped in surplus cheese as well—"disaster cheese," the village kids called it.

The brooding sky, the black raven, the dark spruce: I drive into a dim foreboding, a light sadness brought on by thinking about Smitty, his accomplishments, what he has learned that I would like to know, and his prospects for a short life. Thinking of Smitty reminds me of others I've known whose lives have been too short. This is not as heavy a matter as it sounds, perhaps, for over time one learns to live with losses. But it leads to wonder: Does the bleakness of this landscape, as I see it now, foster a bleakness in my thoughts about Smitty? How much does the land create our reality for us? On another day, would a similar landscape lead to exultation? I have no answers to these questions when Smitty steps down from his low front porch to greet me.

We talk about old friends in the bay, and the conversation turns to myths and legends we have heard: the stories of moss men told by Indians along the shores of Lake Iliamna; the stick men of the Athapaskans along the Upper Kuskokwim and the Yukon; the bear stories and stories of giants and the "little black men who live underground" told by schoolchildren in Bristol Bay. Smitty's experience at this time is far wider than mine, and I'm always a student in his presence.

My own students, and the elders in villages around the bay, have told me stories involving bears, and Smitty has heard many of them. I suggest it is because the great Alaska brown bear, a summer resident in great numbers, plays such an important role in the lives of people there. Smitty points out that our people have bear stories too—"All of them lies, of course," he grins. We talk about Hugh Glass. He has read Frederick Manfred's novel *Lord Grizzly* and loves it as I do. "I can't believe how a guy could turn a wilderness adventure into a parable about redemption and forgiveness," Smitty says, "and spin out all the complex threads of our obligations to one another." Once he started to write down all the bear stories he'd heard up here, but he says, "The collection was lost while I was away soldiering during the Korean War," and he never tried to gather them again. He gets out his books and we compare notes on artifacts. "This point is just like the ones an Eskimo guy in Shaktoolik still uses hunting seals," Smitty claims.

Outside, the snow piles up, white and pristine and soft. Inside Smitty's cabin it is warm, easy, stimulating. The wood fire occasionally splats or pops, and the cabin smells of burning spruce and the spiced Russian tea that steeps on the table. To all appearances Smitty is feeling fine, but when the afternoon is nearly gone, we finally talk about the issues our conversation has delicately evaded and delayed. Smitty says he will be going to Anchorage again, to the hospital, in a few days. They will begin some kind of therapy for his back and check again for his cancer. "Just routine," he insists. The old cancer had been in his lymph system, and he had had x-ray treatments. He speaks of these things as if they were a matter of no concern, but I have had other friends with cancer, and none of them had survived a cancer that had become a lymphoma, and it seems that a kind of tension has moved in behind his apparently offhand words.

As Smitty talks I realize that he knows the cancer is back and out of fear has been stalling about seeing the doctor again. He does not want his own understanding confirmed. Further, I realize that he knows I have guessed and has therefore been trying to make the afternoon pleasant and easy for me. But my presence should be repugnant to him, my health an affront to his illness, my underlying optimism an affront to his reality. Why doesn't he shout, shake his fist, curse his fate, take issue with the life that has been given him, I wonder.

I say that I have to be in Anchorage while he is in the hospital and will stop by to see him. I don't really have any commitments, at least at the moment, but I have to put it that way because Smitty has a certain pride. If I'd said I was coming just to see him, he would have protested the distance, the icy roads, denied the implied caring.

Since I have said I have to be in town anyway, he seems pleased by the idea and encourages it. I suppose such deceit is wrong, but this is just another in our own little series of mutual deceits, the kind we have been dancing with all afternoon, and under them lies a certain understanding. We each know what the other is doing. Is it, then, really a deceit? Whatever it is, it is a matter of courtesy not to call one another on it. Perhaps for us courtesy is more important than the truth. We know we cannot escape it anyway. Truth, knowing nothing of courtesy, will force itself on us. So we dance our little dance of courtesy, not to evade or deny the truth but to keep it in its place for a time. Sooner or later, we know, we'll get around to saying everything that needs to be said.

Anxiety spins my wheels in the soft new snow of his lane as

I leave. My mind frets at our closing conversation, the inadequacy I feel in the face of his struggle, the sadness at the prospects for his immediate future, the possibility that his life will end soon, perhaps in pain. Although I am a coward, I feel that I would take his suffering upon myself but that there is no way, and if there were a way, deep down I know I would not take it. I am glad to be myself and not him. I have said all that I can honestly say: that I will visit him in the hospital. The bottom of the car leaves grooves in the new snow as I drive through the trees along his lane, lurch up onto the gravel road that leads to the highway, and switch on the headlights.

Once a week through the winter I follow the twisting narrow road from Kenai to Anchorage to see Smitty, sometimes sneaking in verboten cigarettes, occasionally a milk shake, always taking books. He loves Norman Chance's book *The Eskimo of North Alaska,* thinks it accurate and useful to folks other than anthropologists. On one visit he commented that good scholarship in anthropology, history, the various sciences, and even literature was much more pragmatic for Alaskans than for folks in the Lower 48. "We need to know that stuff," he says, "just to get through the week up here, especially if you live outside Anchorage and Fairbanks, which every real Alaskan does," he adds, and then laughs, turning his self-righteousness back on himself. I had invited Mary along a couple of times when I was headed in to town, but she declined for unstated reasons that had nothing to do with schedule—she didn't simply say, "I've got another commitment today"—so I did not press but told her that if she ever wanted to go, she could give me a call.

At seven tonight Smitty's nurse called from Providence Hospital in Anchorage to say that if I wanted to see Smitty alive, I'd better get there tonight. And could I somehow bring his wife along, please? Mary has not been there in the five months since Smitty was admitted. I have a meeting this evening, one I cannot get out of because there are no phones south of Soldotna yet and I can't let folks know I won't be there. I promise the nurse I'll get there as soon as I can and then call Mary and tell her the circumstances. She immediately agrees to come, and I agree to pick her up as soon as possible, warning her it will be late.

On the way to the small cabin on Coho Beach Road where Mary lives, I hear the car radio announce that the highway is blocked by snowslides along Turnagain Arm between Girdwood and Anchorage, but the plows are working on it. We are 160 mostly crooked, mostly mountainous miles from there, and it is the only road. I calculate the time, the driving through this thick-falling snow on these slick roads, and believe that if we can get away from Mary's by 11:30 or midnight, enough time will have passed for the plows to have opened the road before we get to Girdwood. We can squirt through and be in Anchorage by 4:00 or 4:30 in the morning. There is an element of luck in-volved in such an estimate, of course, and I always tend to tout the odds in my favor. There is a stretch from Gwin's to Gird-wood, for example, a distance of perhaps sixty-five miles, where nothing is apt to be open if we should have trouble. Kenai Bob's, Sunrise Inn, and the roadhouse at Summit Lake are the only establishments along the road, and they all close when the bar closes for the winter months. The fact that the cabins always have at least one open door for travelers in distress is no help. Our need is to get to town, and stopping short of our goal makes it all hopeless. Why I calculate this way I don't know. Gwin's probably won't be open either.

Near midnight I pull into the lane where Mary lives. New snow cascades up over the car's bumper and headlights in a great white spray. The yard light is on, the snow yellowing as it swirls in the light. Mary bundles up and gets in my station wagon. We drive back to the highway without getting stuck, talking about Smitty, speculating about what we might find when we see him.

Both of us turn thoughtful and inward at the prospect, drop into silence. Mary finally dozes and I concentrate on the road.

Snowflakes drift hugely into the headlights. The highway across the flat that marks the Kenai burn is straight and level. Two moose, eyes glowing red in my headlights as they materialize wraithlike out of the flurries, climb from the bar pit on my right. I dim the lights and they lumber off to the other side and jog out of sight. In the little cut through the rocks of a lateral moraine just before Sunrise Inn, another moose is on the road and has no room to move. I stop in time and wait. He turns back, lurches stiff-legged and tall around the high rocks and down a steep incline and disappears into the trees along Kenai Lake.

Since the beginning of October, the highway has been snow packed and icy. Once I slid sideways through the tight turn along the Kenai River just south of Gwin's while a semi came through it from the other direction. I can still see the driver's jaw dropping as we passed, my radiator inches from the side of his van, my headlights blasting its black tires and white side, his gaping mouth pasted against the glass. He passed in a white roar, kicking up a veil of snowdust just as the back end of my Chevy spun into his lane. At the end of my 360 I was back in the right lane and awake enough so I no longer needed to stop at Gwin's for coffee.

Once a moose reversed himself in the road and turned back toward the car just as I passed, unable to stop. His nose just bumped the sidepost near my eye as his head swung around. His face looked eight feet long. My frequent trips mean that (1) I know this road in intimate detail and in all kinds of weather, (2) the blinding snow tonight is less a problem than if the road were unfamiliar, (3) that I have a good idea where the moose (creatures of habit) hang out, and (4) that I therefore drive too fast.

As we descend from Turnagain Pass down the long sidehill curves that slant to Turnagain Arm, the snow turns to freezing rain and along the arm it is raining hard. The mountains on our right are obscured, and the wrack and scrabble of ice on the arm itself is visible for only a few yards before it fades into a silver-black scrim of rain and mist. The arm was named by Captain James Cook, who sailed up here looking for a Northwest Passage from this side of the continent. The arm grew shallow and forced him back. Discouraged at still another blind canyon in the ocean—part of the sullen impermeability of our continent's western coast—he marked his chart "Turn Again."

At Girdwood the plows are pulling back into the highway department garages, their headlights the eyes of surreal yellow insects. My guess has proved right: the avalanche was small, the plows have done their work, and the road is clear. We make the sharp turn west over the railroad tracks and I accelerate. Abruptly, around the next bend I drive into an avalanche that must have come down just behind the plows. It is not possible to stop; the Chevy rides up on the snow and settles. Snow is up to the windows on both sides and we cannot open either door, but we are okay.

We are in a very safe place. The precarious snow on the high ridges, undermined by the thaw, is already down in this spot. A second avalanche in exactly the same place is unlikely. I switch off the engine and get the sleeping bags out of the back seat so we can stay warm, and we settle down to wait. There seems little to say. There has not been a car on the road for more than two hours, so we may be here a while.

Half an hour later a semi pulls up across from us, headlights in our faces, blinding after the darkness. The road to Anchorage must be open to that point. He cannot turn around on this narrow, pot-holed road, still gravel after the earthquake took it out a couple of years before, but he could back up. I crawl over the seats, roll down the station wagon's rear window, and make my way across the rubble to the semi cab.

I stand in the cold rain, shouting to make my request heard over the diesel's rumbling idle. The driver says no, he has no chain to pull me out and that I should get up in his cab, it is crazy to be out there, and even if he did have a chain he wouldn't get out to get it because it is safer to be in the cab if there is another slide. I tell him he doesn't have to get out, just tell me where the chain is and I'll hook up. All he has to do is back up and yank me over. I do not believe he has no chain; no trucker makes that run down the Kenai in winter without one. My story of our urgency, a soon-to-be-widow's plight (I am shameless with my story), does not sway him. I do not want to call him a liar, but it is tempting to go to the tool box alongside his cab and get the chain. But the box is probably locked, and then, if it weren't, I'd need him to back up, and I suspect he wouldn't, so I bag the notion and go back to the car. The semi is huge, I tell Mary, warmer, should be safe, . . .

We clamber over the seats and out the back window, scramble over the slide, and hoist ourselves up the rungs into the semi's cab. The heater's blast induces sleep. We both want to nap, but the driver wants to talk, feeling compelled, apparently, to tell us just how dangerous our situation is. He is full of stories about disasters along this stretch of road. Just a year ago along here, he tells us, he lost a friend: "Whole semi just wiped away into Turnagain Arm by this snow slide, see, just like this one. He was parked like we are, couldn't turn around, and a second one came down, washed him right out to sea. Can't ever tell where they're apt to come," he says, or when, and he's "not getting out to help nobody. Even if a big one comes right down here, we're better off in this cab." The danger is only moderately real; everything else is just talk.

Another half an hour and I see lights come down out of the trees across the arm, a trucker bound for Anchorage, snow and our car blocking his path. He pulls up across the little avalanche from us. I go over to see if he has a chain. Sure, he allows. I hook up and he backs up so slowly and gently that we are pulled with no damage up and out of the snow and back onto the highway. But we are still on the wrong side of the slide and cannot get to Anchorage. It is 4:00 A.M., and the plows won't be out again till six. We are only forty minutes from Anchorage, so it is better, we decide, to wait here than to drive four hours back to Kenai.

Whether the commuter planes will fly in this freezing rain is doubtful.

I get Mary from the semi's cab and we drive back to the pullout at Girdwood and try to get comfortable and sleep. Before I doze off I see a white cloud boiling behind the Anchorage semi. A bright flare of blue sparks lights it, a brief moment of electric blue brilliance as the high-tension wires snap and the poles go down. Mary is already asleep.

At six the plows pass us on their way to clear the road. The slide we were in is quickly cleared. The chainless semi roars past us, headed down the peninsula the way we've come. We cross the tracks again, see our slide parted like the Red Sea, and, spirits picking up, press on. Two miles later we are stopped by a flagman. The plows are working ahead of us in a deep cut where the highway crosses a ridge. We face a wall of snow four stories high, with yellow maintenance vehicles like toys at its base. A supervisor walks back to tell us it will take all day to clear it.

We turn around and drive back to Kenai through the grayest dawn I've ever seen. When I phone from the airport in Kenai, the hospital says Smitty is still alive but it can't be long. The next plane to Anchorage is at 11:00. We take it, rent a car, and arrive at the hospital about noon to find Smitty conscious and grinning. He is pleased, touched, to see Mary. It is a matter of seconds for tears, pats, a long history of alternating closeness and estrangement, intimacy and distance, to become reconciliation. Smitty stays awake and is strong enough to talk. I leave them to it and go downstairs to the coffee shop.

Smitty is still alive that night and Mary and I wait. She is shocked for she has not witnessed the decline as Smitty's body has withered to eighty-five pounds. At midnight the nurses wheel in another bed and Mary lies down for a while. We wait. Next morning Smitty has a few moments when he is awake enough to talk. "Could sure use a cigarette," he grins, "but the nurses would have a fit." His coughs waste him, he slips into a deep coma. At two the following morning, Mary at his side and me sleeping at the home of friends, Smitty gives it up.

When we think of the renewal the land provides for our spirits, what comes to mind are magnificent vistas, grand colors in sky or rock, the sudden intensity of wild animals encountered. But what could provide a more intimate connection with the earth than digging a grave for a friend? Back down on the peninsula it has turned cold. Four of us are trying to dig Smitty's grave. There is no undertaker on the Kenai yet and no city services out here, so we have to do this ourselves. The ground is frozen and the going is slow. Spindly birch and scraggly spruce surround us; what light there is, is gray.

We use axes, picks, shovels. We alternate swinging the axe and the pick, and spell each other shoveling out the debris. Smitty's body is coming back tomorrow morning, will be flown down from Anchorage to the airport in Kenai. A couple of friends will pick him up. They won't need help; he won't be heavy. The funeral will be in the afternoon. We have arranged for pallbearers, written an obituary, reserved the church, made up an order of service. The women have talked among themselves and will bring cookies, cakes, and coffee. They have done this before and know that folks will linger a long time.

Bob Nelson, the Methodist preacher for the Kenai parish and a friend of Smitty's, will conduct the service. Irreverent about everything, Smitty had helped Bob put the homemade stained glass windows into the little church at Tustumena when it was built, and though it must have hurt him, he helped me and a couple of others crib up the cesspool. The rest of us will take part in the service too, reading scripture or prayers, talking about Smitty, cobbling up our homemade ceremonial. Afterward we will sit around eating too many cookies, drinking too much coffee, talking through the afternoon and into the evening. We will reminisce, and laugh so hard at some of the stories that tears will stream down our faces. Out of our foolish laughter and considerable high irreverence of our own (it will seem perfectly appropriate in the light slanting through the stained glass), a kind of comfort will settle with the darkness, and we will go home.

For now we work and sweat and freeze. We talk about Smitty and tell outrageous jokes and remember the time he did this or that. Under the byline Coho Smith he used to write an occasional column for the *Kenai Clarion,* our weekly paper. Bud Keener, a fellow fisherman, remembers the time Smitty noted that the highway department "had made preparations to give the road away again." In other places, he wrote, when they stuck those little red ribbons down the middle of the road it meant that it was going to be repaired, maybe even paved. Our rough gravel road had had so many ribbons pinned on it so many times only to have nothing happen. All we could assume was that it was gradually being gift wrapped and they were going to give it away at Christmas.

White birch trunks and snow are darkened by occasional spruce in this mixed thicket. Under the snow are blueberries and cranberries, still blue and red. The woods around us have gone still in the still air. We become quiet too as the work goes on and we drift into the mental slack tide between our earlier hilarity and the inevitable tide swing after. Only an occasional raven's squawk and our own heavy breathing interrupt the silence. The nearest community seems far away. Every place alive and civilized and brightly lighted seems far away. The sun, pale and low all day, goes behind the trees; the cold deepens.

There is a clearing a mile from here marking a field where a homesteader failed to make it. I can see in my mind the four moose that have grazed in it every afternoon this winter. I am sure they are there, will be out of the trees by now, black and stately at the field's edge.

The talk picks up again, the weight of memory, perhaps, drawing us back to company, the camaraderie of survivors working and joking to contain themselves, trying to do right by a friend as the northern world goes dark.

THE DRYLAND FARMER

I awake in heat more proper to midday, shower, and drive
north on Montana 401, then turn off and take back roads up to
Molt and over to Rapelje. There are wheat strips to the east,
west, north, and south. The grain elevators rise above the prairie
like gothic cathedrals above the plains of France. The sun in this
early morning strikes their pale columns, gleaming like mirrors
off their conical roofs. This is antelope country too, and the sun
strikes the antelopes' white rumps, making bright dots visible
from so far away that it is not possible to make out an animal at
all, the white glare off the erectile rump hair the only sign that a
creature is there. The tawny back and neck blend perfectly with
the landscape. The dots are scattered along one sidehill and despite the distance they will have no trouble seeing me. Their eyes
are far sharper than mine and, biologists say, can pick out a stationary object ten inches in diameter over a mile away. More
than once I have pulled out binoculars to see if those light spots
were really antelope, only to find them standing stock still looking at me when I finally found the focus.

Dryland farming is the norm in country like this, barley or
winter wheat growing in green strips alternating with strips of
summer fallow, beige stubble, and dark soil stretching from horizon to horizon. The land is not as flat as it seems, and antelope

can disappear in its protective folds as if behind a magician's cape. Like the land, there are nuances to some dryland farmers, and not everything about them may be open to view. For nearly thirty years now I've been lucky to know a few such men, and their wives, and I find myself lost in reverie in this morning light, remembering old friends I've admired. All of them have worked at hard physical labor from their earliest years; none have a college education. All of them find deep pleasure in knowing their fields and streams, and joy in lives that are often hard, always complex, and frequently painful.

If you are going to have trouble of almost any kind, from a car with a busted tie-rod to a dying parent or a child gone wrong, these folks make valued companions. Indeed, one reason I've cherished them for years, even when we've been out of touch for long periods, is the sense that every time I'm with them I'm going to learn something about my life that my college education never taught me. And when I watch them wrestle with the pain and chaos that strike us all, the mutuality of our human experience and the memory of my own floundering around under similar circumstances establish ties that cannot be broken by mere distance or time away.

These farm folk are just as apt as anyone else to have a powerful intellectual life. In fact, that intellectual life is deeply rooted in the fundamental human questions that we all fret about and worry through, the very questions that the ancient Greeks, and the wise elders of every tribe before and since, have sought to answer.

The couple I'd like you to meet, Sherm and Mary, are a composite—not fictional, because everything I attribute to them I have experienced firsthand with some western farm couple, but they are, strictly speaking, an invention.

I've hunted antelope with Sherm more than once in the very country I'm driving through now. The rolling prairie, flat-topped buttes, and level stretches of the plains give us a long view of the land. Once, just at dawn, we saw a band of antelope and left the pickup at the edge of this gravel road and headed in their direction. It would be sunup and legal to shoot by the time we had made our stalk. Not once did those antelope seem alarmed, yet they drifted slowly before us, always keeping about the same distance away. We never did catch up, and when, finally tired and ready to give up, we simply stood up and walked without guile or pretense directly at them, they ran down into one of those mysterious folds in the earth we could not even see three quarters of a mile away and never appeared again. We looked around, shrugging off our concentration on the animals and the terrain as if we had been drugged, and discovered that we were about four miles from the truck. We trudged back to the vehicle, a dry, mostly uphill hike against the grade, climbing vaguely toward the Continental Divide.

After an hour or so, Sherm said, "What are we hunting?" His voice sounded as if it were a serious question.

"Antelope," I said, my head down, scuffing along. "Why?"

"Look," he said, laughing. There, perhaps fifty yards away, just behind us on the right, eleven antelope trotted single-file along a ridge in full view. We both laughed so hard at the ironies inherent in that scene that neither of us bothered to shoot.

Sherm drives two hundred miles to a town of 55,000 to trade in his pickup, and he shops while he is there, but I've never known him to take the extra time to go to the library, a play, or a concert. If he goes to a theater, which is unlikely, it will be to see a movie, not a play.

What Sherm and Mary know of history is what they learned in elementary and secondary school thirty-five years ago. Their knowledge of the Civil War got a boost recently from TV, and history came to their attention again last week because the superintendent fired the social studies teacher and they learned that history is now a part of that larger field.

They also know very closely where the animals are for ten or more square miles around their place: the deer in that coulee three miles south of the house and that other one just west; the huns (Hungarian partridges) in that stubble field you can see from the living room window; the family of red fox denned up behind that ridge above the house, the one that fails to keep the north wind at bay. There are two fox parents and three kits, and Sherm and Mary know that one kit has a withered left foreleg. They also know how to stitch up the cow with a prolapse and give shots to the mare they still use in country too rough for the pickup, and just how the winter wheat will be affected by these extra days of furnace heat from a sun too relentless to make room for rain and how that will affect their chances at the bank next fall. Sherm can calculate in his head the acre-feet of water he'll need for the wheat in that new patch he rented and can judge the ditch contour exactly so that the ditch he builds will provide the coverage he needs.

What Sherm does, he usually does passing well. He'll put a new transmission in his truck and it will run fine. He'll fix his tractor too, with help from his son, because it saves money and because he can't take the time to get it to town and wait till someone else fixes it for him, and he couldn't afford it anyway. If something has to be welded, he has the equipment and he will weld it. If he needs a building, he can lay it out on paper, frame it, floor it, side it, and roof it, then plumb it, wire it, and paint it. Though it may not quite fit the city code, it will last for three generations.

On the day when Sherm is in the lumberyard trying to find a few straight studs and some plywood, and the millhand comes around back to tell him he has a phone call, Sherm's heart does the same little jump yours or mine would. And when I'm driving and listening to Sherm consider his father, who has just suffered a massive heart attack, he goes back over the same questions anyone would.

"He's been pretty temperate," Sherm says, thinking about his dad's chances, "though he used to tie one on pretty good, years back, just on weekends." After a pause, "We sure had our differences. He didn't want Mary and me to get married, no way, but after he seen what a fine wife she made, he came around. . . . I hope Ben can keep him alive till I get there. Mary said both he and Doc Kane are working on him. If anybody can do anything, they can." He adds, shaking his head, "He was a good hand," the ultimate accolade. Mary had said on the phone that they need blood, and I volunteer. "Good," he says, "he needs some that's got a lot of fish and venison in it." Sherm's reflections are a mix of memory and assessment, combining memories of the past with prospects for the future. This is not an intellectual exercise, of course, and does not reflect any particular wisdom. But for most of us, trying to get to the hospital before our father dies, weighing the chances, and thinking back over a life well or poorly spent is not an intellectual exercise either, and wisdom under such pressure is generally scarce amongst us all.

The luckiest among us get to work at the tasks that fascinate us. Learning how another day of sun will affect the wheat, or where the dough must sit to rise just right, or how to grind the valves to a perfect fit is appropriate human knowledge. The discipline required to achieve such knowledge is similar for us all, and the product is not to be scorned. Further, we all ponder the impossible-to-answer in an immediate way, for we all suffer and we all think about those larger matters that puzzle and confuse us when life goes painfully awry and pat answers won't suffice. We all grope toward meaning for our lives in both personal and public spheres. Here is common ground between our average urban selves and the average rancher of any kind. What Sherm wants to know is

> how to get along with his wife and kids, his parents, and his brothers, cousins, nephews, and nieces who live on ranches scattered around the region; and

> how to help his decaying community, population 168, survive and prosper. It suffered a serious economic blow when the schools were consolidated in a nearby town, and it also lost a major portion of its identity in the process. Now even the grain elevator may close. And

> how to make a living as a dryland farmer. He does not wish to dominate the land, as some environmentalists

and intellectuals seem to believe. He learned long ago the fatuous impossibility of that. But, yes, like the biblical Jacob, he is in a kind of wrestling match with the earth and the gods. He wants less to control the earth than to establish a liaison with it, perhaps even a relationship. He knows that the relationship will always be tentative, fragile, and easily broken, but it should be one that acknowledges that there is room for him to live on the earth, that will let him and his wife and their children create a life on the land. He wants a place on the land because he would rather be there than anywhere else, and he works to keep it, quoting his father's instructions about grazing cattle on the bench he homesteaded: "Take half and leave half, and you'll always have grass."

He thinks about

why his niece, who is beautiful, eighteen, intelligent, articulate, gentle, and already engaged has been stricken with a virus that will confine her to a wheelchair for the rest of her life; and

why his oldest son—who loves nothing more than driving a tractor from before dawn until after dark, watching the rows drift behind the Farmall as carefully as Sherm watches the drift of a dry fly, watching with the same intensity and concentration that transports one out of one's own mind into another consciousness—why such a young man had to learn to shoot a machine gun out the open side of a helicopter gunship in a place as far away as Southeast Asia; and

why his son, or any young man, should have to watch his closest friend get shot and then dangle from a strap to haul his gut-shot companion up, leaving intestines, blood, bile, and feces draped and dripping over the runners on which the ship will eventually land.

When his son writes home from Viet Nam and tells Sherm fragments of such experiences and asks why these things have to happen, Sherm has no answer. He was never in combat himself, but the rest of his life Sherm will see his brother Dean squatting in a corner of the shop, fingers in his mouth, moaning in terror because they are attacking him. They are North Koreans. When we finally take his brother from the bunkhouse where he is crouched behind the bed with all his guns arrayed before him, ready to kill the attackers of his imagination as they come through the bunkhouse door, and when we have checked Dean into the VA hospital some two hundred miles away and there is nothing more we can do but turn away and go home, Sherm weeps without embarrassment for his brother's pain and confusion. He wants to know what he could have done that would have made it easier for Dean. Now, twenty-five years later, the images of that time are fresh, and at odd moments he wonders if his son, too, will one day cower in some corner, imagination aflame, under attack.

He wonders

why his neighbor, never sick a day in his life, must die at the age of thirty-six, leaving a wife and four children; and

why another neighbor, to the east, gets caught by medical bills and sinks so far into debt that he loses the ranch he worked so hard to own for eighteen years.

And he wants to know

where the courage comes from to keep on going despite such setbacks, the kind of courage exemplified by his poverty-bound neighbor's wife, who, on seeing her husband come in for breakfast with his shirt and pants covered with fresh wet manure acquired patching up a cow with a prolapse, said, "Well, Tom, I don't mind being rich, but I hate being stinking rich," and laughed as she helped her husband out of his clothes.

And he thinks about

> how to get an extra five bushels of barley per acre out
> of his stony soil, and why his father, who was a good
> enough man, must die a painful and lingering death,
> unable to quit this life even though he is ready to. Why
> does that labored breathing continue on the thin edge
> between pain and darkness when it is for no purpose?

Sherm ponders these things, as you and I ponder similar
events in our own lives, while also trying to grind the valves on
his tractor before planting, and fixing its transmission as fast as
possible when it breaks down in the midst of harvest. He wonders about these things at the same time that he wonders

> how to get the school board to extend its bus route to
> pick up his kids; and

> what to do for Peter Emich, the elderly Dutch immi-
> grant whose wife just died; and

> how to persuade the county commissioners that the
> bridge over Sage Creek is dangerous and that the pro-
> posed tax levy will be an impossible burden; and

> why government is always infernally foolish and stub-
> born; and

> what some midwestern farmer, suddenly made secre-
> tary of agriculture, can possibly know about dryland
> farming when he goes to Congress with a new farm bill
> that is great for those who raise cows for milk but stu-
> pid for those who raise them for beef and that takes no
> account of barley and wheat at all.

Sherm's wife also wonders about these things, of course, and
they talk about them over coffee when Sherm comes in from
the barn on midmornings in winter, or on Sunday during dinner before Sherm watches the football game and Mary does the

dishes, or in the pickup driving to the state basketball tournament. Both of these folks, traveling through the dark in the dashboard glow behind the headlights, are intellectuals, and if I speak too much here from Sherm's point of view and too little from Mary's, it is not because her point of view is less important. It is because our western life freely permits emotional and intellectual intimacies between men, while it is not the custom to drop by the ranch and hang around the kitchen for hours on end with another man's wife while her husband is absent. So men tend to spend more time with men—working, fixing things, hunting or fishing—than they do with women and have more to report from that point of view.

It is life, not learning, that thrusts Sherm and Mary into considering the fundamental issues of life's purpose and meaning. Though they think deeply, when they talk about the most serious issues they won't bedeck the conversation with garlands of quotations from Socrates or Plato, and they won't have read Montaigne or know the dramatic story of Oedipus or be familiar with most of the references that enrich the professional scholar's dialogue and which some hold to be the common glue of discourse that holds a culture together. Instead, they'll tell a little story about their neighbor, or they'll relate what they saw once while Sherm was looking for strays, or they'll cite what Tom said when his pa died, or the way the preacher talked about it, and what they thought of that, and why he was all wrong. These are the stories that are the common glue of discourse, and when one is fortunate enough to be present, those conversations are as rich and stimulating as any, the stories right to the point and somehow comforting.

Sherm uses his intellect as we all do, bringing it to bear as best he can when life demands it. When up against the real issues, both Sherm and Mary will marshal every reference, relevant and irrelevant, and then sort it all through, sifting the evidence of both experience and knowledge, and worry it out till the answer that they need in order to avoid despair, or to live with it, emerges. People who are far better educated, myself included, also grope toward tentative answers to the tough questions that arise when life strikes us a hard blow, and our answers, too, are often couched in language that is fumbling, stories that are simple and homespun, and assertions that are made without great confidence.

SHEEP-DIP

At the end of the first week of August, I leave Salt Lake at 5:30 in the morning, heading north on my way to eastern Oregon. The moon is still pale and full in the lightening sky, the sun already up but not yet above the mountain barrier to the east, the air still cool and pleasant. But just to the west the dry mountains rise to the early light. It burns their tops an ominous fiery red, and it is already clear that shortly after noon the temperature will again be in the high 90s. Antelope Island floats in a beige haze, appears so hot and barren that if one were on its shore, it would seem wise to launch bottles with messages immediately.

A few miles north of Sweetzer Summit (across the border into Idaho), Raft River is all weeds, no water, a shallow depression in a wide swathe through the fields, the banks so over-cropped that they have less vegetation than the course where the river used to run. It has been this way for years, and the river is not coming back.

I am not one of those who believe that we ought to get all the cattle off all the public lands. We need to become wise enough to make distinctions, to keep permits in the hands of those who use them wisely and out of the hands of those who abuse them. But I am sure the rancher who allowed this destruction must be out of business by now, for such practice destroys the future, and in a sudden moment of meanness I am glad he's gone. It's cheaper to support him and his family on welfare than on permits that cost the land so dearly.

East of Hayburn two combines are harvesting on one side of the highway; on the other, white potato blossoms point to a later harvest, and a little red Massey-Ferguson is cutting stubble for straw. Farther west the bright yellow strips of wheat alternate with the dark green of potatoes and beans. In this landscape, composed mostly of pale pastels, these colors are so vivid they shock the system. No wonder Van Gogh lost his mind among the sunflowers at Arles.

As this open Idaho country drops toward the Snake, a rock escarpment lifts above the river on the southwest side. Alluvial ridges falling from its limestone outcrop barely have time to spread in a small fan before hitting the bottom. A crop duster spraying fields swoops low, spooking a flock of mallards in the river. For an instant the yellow plane and the ducks are on the same level, wheeling away from each other, the plane climbing in unnatural defiance of stall angle, and the ducks, only fifty yards above the water, already drawing into their neat natural V. They lift away, becoming lost against the gray sagebrush and rocks, and an image swims into mind: Michael Baring-Gould leaping from his front porch near Wasilla, Alaska, arms wide, great face split by a huge, lopsided grin, to shout hello and give me a customary Michael hug. At his memorial service a number of us commented on the hug, and the grin. Joe E. Brown would have said, "It could swallow a banana—sideways."

Where do such images come from? Nothing I can think of that happened yesterday or thus far today had reminded me of Michael. Thinking of him, others crowd to mind: Guy Groat coasting over the house in Naknek, the sky thick with fog, the landing strip he's headed for not yet visible to him, the ridge that will rear up to pull his plane down and apart still unseen ahead; Carol, her car smashed and leaking blood; Pop, his chest lifting and falling in a body that will soon do even less; Coho and Zeck, Kathryn, Harold, and Tom.

One image is of the Red Lodge Cafe and Tom Olcott finishing his first cup of coffee and banging his heavy mug down on the counter within a quarter-inch of the hand of the waitress who was leaning there visiting with us. She did not flinch or pull her hand away or even change her tone of voice. "Pretty steady," said Tom. "I'll have another shot of sheep-dip." Slowly she straightened, pulled her hands from the counter, and turned to the coffee urn. Tom was a regular. He had his own coffee mug, kept on a special shelf behind the counter with ten or twelve similar cups used mostly by other businessmen of Tom's generation. Several of them made it to the cafe at about the same time each weekday morning, and they would drink and jibe each other and trade the news or the gossip, depending on which was juicier. Sometimes they told old stories they'd all heard before. The mugs had been glazed with a special cartoon appropriate for each man and paid for by Charlie Stevens, who owned the place.

Tom's had his name on it, and a cartoon joke stolen from Digger O'Dell, the undertaker on *Fibber McGee and Molly*: "I'll be the last friend to let you down." Tom had been the undertaker in Red Lodge for twenty-some years, and if he had ever been enchanted with his task, he was no longer. He was now of an age to be burying people he had known all his life: mentors, fellow poker players, longtime business associates, hunting partners. Hardest of all, perhaps, were the funerals for children of his old friends. Those came more often than one might think. When the fourteen-year-old son of his best friend died, all six of the pallbearers, all old friends of Tom's, were men who had lost a child of their own.

An hour before the funeral for Harold Wood, Tom was at the church, making final arrangements of the flowers, fussing with the casket. The soloist, a young preacher from Bridger, was rehearsing with the organist. Tom took out his wallet and stuffed fifty dollars into John's hand as payment for his singing. The usual fee those days was ten.

Harold was a gentleman, much like my father. Both were of a kind common to that pre–World War I generation and now gone or anachronistic: midwestern farm boys, ten or eleven when the Great War came, adults after it was over. They did a man's work from the age of ten and helped with chores, many of them heavy, long before that. They moved off the farm and into white-collar jobs in town during the Depression, grew mildly urbane in demeanor, using their English carefully so as not to be mistaken for a country boy, courteous in every situation, graceful and witty in mixed company, a man when among men, competent at a hundred tasks, few of which matter anymore. Whatever urbanity they achieved was always tempered with the quiet pragmatism and humor required by farm life. When I was in college, a biology prof remarked that women did not need to use the many cosmetic chemicals on their faces to give themselves beautiful complexions, that they could accomplish the same end by washing twice a day with plain soap and water and staying outdoors as much as possible, getting plenty of sunshine. I reported his comment to Pop and he replied, straight-faced, "Maybe, but I never met a farmer I wanted to kiss."

Tom was a western variation on the same theme, what both Harold and my dad would have called "a rough diamond": raconteur, gambler, all sharp corners and unexpected turns, hardworking, hard-headed, and soft-hearted, a marvelous wing shot, irreverent and irrepressible. He once explained to me how we could double the attendance and quadruple the collection at the Methodist church by installing a slot machine in the church foyer. Some said he had run through several fortunes, making money and losing it in a big way. Others who grew up with him said that when Tom was a young man, delivering wholesale groceries, he could carry a hundred-pound sack of flour on each shoulder, the soft flour conforming to his wide body without need of additional support while he carried another in his hands.

Tom and Harold had hunted together, partied together, and belonged to the Elks, the Rotary, and the Inquiry Club. In the thirties Tom and a few other men from Red Lodge had hunted deer in the Little Belt Mountains, opening up new trails in that country, hunting in bitter cold and snow, always nosing around the same ridges and meadow edges, exploring new canyons, the last week of each season, year after year, always staying at Bill Korrell's ranch.

Harold had not participated in those hunts for some time, but the year he retired he went back up and stayed the week. I drove him there one night, stopping once in Harlowton for supper and again on the prairie north of Harlowton so we could both get out and stare in amazement and delight at a ground blizzard aswirl and blinding in the headlights. Miles from any ranch, standing up on the bumper in the wind, we could see the cloudless sky and myriad stars while the snow blasted against our legs and snagged at our jackets.

Harold did not get a deer that year and did not care. What he wanted was to be again with those men, to be out in those hills—so new now after all those years, and so familiar. It was a great nostalgia tonic for him. They hunted during the day, jeeping around the old trails they had invented, ate like horses at the Korrells' table, had a drink in the evening. Their rule was that after you'd touched a drink, you couldn't touch a gun, and if you made such a move, they'd call you on it. They swapped yarns about the days when they hunted practically alone in those hills and had the whole country to themselves.

A year after Harold's last hunt he was dead of a heart attack suffered while on a trip to Europe, a trip he did not want but was willing to make because his wife wanted it and he wanted to please her. He and Grace had come home in stages: a relapse in England, and another, fatal one in Indiana, visiting relatives when they thought Harold was out of danger. At the end, his son-in-law told me later, he murmured over and over, "I want to go home."

The young clergyman looked at the money but knowing that Tom and Harold had been close, said no, he didn't want any money for the singing. Tom looked pained, pushed the fifty dollars back into his hand and growled, "You take it, and you sing, and you sing good!" and walked away.

Can such images spring from a source outside oneself? Does the earth hold not only its own memories but ours as well? Driving through this landscape that has known such losses conjures images of loss in me, becoming the source of images I thought I'd left behind. They seem to fly up like mallards chased off the river by a plane. Why this conjecture about loss unless it is triggered by something around me? Today, what is around me is the land being bashed by colorful machines into food for the table, a few small towns mostly off the road, an occasional truck stop, and blue mountains low on the horizon above miles of sagebrush.

Can it be said that one has gained a loss? We do acquire losses, and the losses grow. Trying to hide them, or ignore them, we pile them up more or less in plain view. The emptiness that appears to define loss builds as the losses grow. But real loss is never emptiness. It does not leave a hole, as many say; it has shape, form, presence, substance. It lies in wait, ready to ambush us when our guard is down. Like an arrow in an old Hollywood western, it thumps silent and unanticipated into our chest. We cannot muster such constant vigilance that we escape its flight nor agility sufficient to evade it.

The sun's glare off this Idaho highway and the yellow stubble has made me drowsy. I'll haul into the Gear Jammer, get some sheep-dip, eyewash, an' squint cure. It's weak, but it will kill mosquitoes and fleas and hold me until I get to Boise, where I can find something strong enough to take care of ticks and lice. Boise will have espresso, which is nature's way of elevating eyelids, opening the whites and rounding the pupils of the eyes. It also manufactures the body's essential plasmas and creates guidance systems for automobiles. Only self-confident folks can drink the stuff; paranoid people know that the sooner they see the whites of yer eyes, the sooner they start to shoot. Tom would have loved it.

Sitting in the booth in this truck stop, I absently ask the waitress for a shot of sheep-dip. She looks blank, says, "What?" Coming to, I repeat myself: "Just a cuppa coffee, please—black."

DEER

Walking a timbered ridge in central Montana's earliest light, I saw, far ahead and below to my right, four mule deer crossing a shadowed meadow. In fact, they were so far away, the light still so dim and their bodies so tiny, I was assuming they were deer by their walk rather than by any clear outline or image. I was guessing they were mule deer too, because in those years whitetails had not taken over the country and preferred brushy lowlands to these arid ridges. The first three, I thought, were does; the last one, trailing a ways behind, might be a buck. Even at that distance, though I could not see antlers, I could guess at gender because bucks move differently from does, and their bodies, especially during the rut, have a somewhat larger and slightly more rectangular silhouette than that of a doe. It is typical, too, of a mule deer buck to hang back for a spell and let the does venture out into a meadow before he enters it himself. If there is danger, the does' fear will reveal it and the buck will not expose himself to it.

These deer were moving on a course that would intersect the ridge I was on. Unless disturbed, they would cross the meadow, perhaps moving to the edge of timber in a small saddle where this ridge tapered off and another began to lift. I had the wind and the trees in my favor and thought I could continue without haste, not spooking other deer that might be unseen between my position and the junction where I expected to cut the deer.

If they crossed the saddle, I knew there was an open coulee and above it another saddle along the ridge to my left—plenty of room to see them if the deer stayed in the open. If they drifted into the trees on my side of the clearing, I had enough time to look around. If I were careful, slow, and quiet enough, I might get a shot before everything came loose and they all bolted. The men I know call this approach pussyfooting, perhaps because we like to imagine ourselves possessed of catlike grace and silence. The sporting magazines, desiring a slightly more elevated tone, call it still-hunting.

The rock over which all hunting breaks is death. Till death is achieved, the hunt remains inconclusive. Only death, or failure and the waning day, ends the pursuit. Death may not be the purpose of the hunt. Death may be the means of achieving a purpose beyond the hunt itself, but it is necessarily embedded in the conclusion of a successful hunt. Because death is inherent in the nature of the hunt, there are two issues each hunter must face: how to justify taking the life of animals and how to hunt without becoming hated by the animals one kills. These are spiritual as well as intellectual tasks.

For some hunters the death of the quarry means little or nothing; the issue is not really considered. For others the hunt is a matter of trophies rather than meat, sport rather than necessity, a chance to test oneself against the animal forces in nature, perhaps. For such hunters the death of an animal may be both celebrated and mourned, but the animal's death is seen as earned by the hunter's effort, exertion, and expense. Many hunters are indifferent to the hunt's outcome. They simply love to be out, to feel themselves participants in a world bright with possibility, beauty, wonder, or surprise. If they get a shot, they will take it; if not, they will not be disappointed. They may hunt happily for years without ever shooting a thing. For still others, hunting is simply a necessity, and the death of animals is an acceptable price to pay for feeding one's family. Some see the hunt, the preparations for it, and the celebrations following as part of a sacred activity, an opportunity to renew or maintain a sense of one's proper place in nature, to practice rituals and procedures handed down from the ancients, to ask permission of the animals before the hunt and forgiveness after. For these, success is not earned but given, and forgiven, and death is not the purpose of the hunt. The purpose is to feed the people, maintain communal and ceremonial life that extends so far back in time we can only dream it, and keep one's relationships in proper balance. Some hunters adopt more than one of these attitudes, holding them in different balances at different times.

To maintain a healthy relationship with the natural world, every culture, except perhaps our present one, established rituals of reciprocal permission, of mutual understanding and forgiveness, to protect the hunter and the people from the displeasure of animals. Perhaps because we now associate the ancient Greeks with city-states, we forget that even they established such rituals. Their dressing of game and disposition of bones followed a ceremonial pattern remarkably similar to that of Aglemute Eskimos, who used to return all the bones of the season's first salmon to the Naknek River. The purpose of such rituals was to assure the game, and ourselves, that it was necessary to take life, that the flesh was not wasted, and that the animal was treated with respect. If the rituals were followed in good faith, the animal would tell his friends and family in the other world that this was a good place, that these were good people. Thus the animals would continue to come, and the village would be fed.

Austin Hammond, a Tlingit elder from Klukwan, once spoke to this issue, saying:

When you shoot a brown bear, his spirit walk away from him and turn to watch you, how you take care of it. You take hemlock branches, or spruce. Before your knife ever touch him, you make a nice bed and roll around in it and then roll bear over on it to work. Then the spirit goes back to its people, and they say, "How is it there?" and he tells them, "Oh, it's nice. They take good care of him." And then the others say, "Then go back there."

Until the moment of death the hunter, the game, and the day may be washed in beauty. After it, no matter how rich the ritual or the understanding, no matter how infused with beauty the day may be, something lies dead and less beautiful. The beauty we ascribe to an animal as we dress it out and prepare it as food is the beauty of memory, whether of animal vitality or courage, of grace or strength or wit, memory of a being that was alive earlier in the day. Though I grew up in a hunting family and had killed many pheasants and ducks, fish and squirrels, cottontails, and a few deer, my first real sense of this came when I was hunting the pine breaks and meadows on this bright day in early fall in the Little Snowy Mountains of central Montana.

Where the timber ran out at the end of the ridge, I looked carefully everywhere but saw neither buck nor does. Where could they have gone? Either they had veered off in another direction, spooked by me or something else, or they had increased their speed or, startled, had broken into a run and passed our expected meeting point before I arrived. Perhaps I had moved too slowly, looking for more certain game. Maybe they had lingered in the timber across the meadow saddle before me.

Just inside the edge of the trees I waited, scanning all the open ground, trying to see into the trees. The slanting light of a rising sun lay in the meadow. The shadows of the last few lodgepole pines stretched across it. On the other side, aspen flared yellow. After minutes I took one step into the open to have a greater range of view and stopped again, watching both meadow and trees for movement—a flick of ear, a step. No deer were visible in the coulee to my left, where they might be if I had taken too much time to get here. I took a few more steps and stopped, then gave up and, thinking the deer gone, decided to walk quickly across the meadow and into the aspen on the far side and continue the hunt along the next ridge.

Halfway across the clearing I looked again, back over my left shoulder, and there, stepping up from the coulee, which was deeper than I had seen, walked the buck. I was standing right out in the open, but he did not seem to care. At the ridge top he turned broadside, directly in line with the sun coming up behind him. He stood there, head high, huge antlers gathering an aura like St. Elmo's magic light, a fiery golden halo around his head. At such a moment imagination, memory, and sight may coalesce. This may in fact be a definition of magic, or of clarity. He was too far away, but I imagined I could see his chest swell with his breath, a muscle twitch under the skin of his shoulder, a tuft of hair on his spine lift in the chill breeze. Light, color, the slightest motion, the faintest sound around me became dream.

In that instant both the deer's life and my own, the trees and the meadow, human and animal, all were alive with beauty, with color and the light's brilliance, and the sibilant wind's soughing. I shot. The deer collapsed without a twitch, was dead before the first echo of my gun came back to me. In the returning stillness and the waning of the dream, the light remained, the pines behind me continued soughing in the breeze, the few aspens ahead ticked and glittered, and the meadow was bathed in color. But the aurora of sun on antler was gone, the richly sensuous life embedded in the moment, a partial eclipse. The deer was not magic but only a deer, and dead. The fleas were already trailing down its legs to seek a warmer life. When I got to the top of the ridge, three does were watching from the far side.

WHITEOUT

The only wisdom we can hope to acquire is the
wisdom of humility. Humility is endless. . . .

—T. S. Eliot

The quality that we call beauty, however, must always
grow from the realities of life, and our ancestors, forced to
live in dark rooms, presently came to discover beauty in
shadows, ultimately to guide shadows towards
beauty's ends. . . . Were it not for shadows
there would be no beauty.

—Jun'ichiro Tanizaki

I t is February and Anchorage is dripping from an unseasonal drizzle. Water runs in the streets, streams off the edges of roofs, pools in the hollows where hard snow lines the sidewalks. I am headed Outside, leaving Anchorage's thaw behind to drive down the Alcan, that rough, twisting highway punched through the wilderness during World War II to link Alaska to America.

Sixty miles out, beyond Sutton, the country lifts into a high canyon. It is colder here, and the rain has turned to thick snow. From Gunsight Lodge, on the high interior tableland beyond the canyon, I drive with my window down in a whiteout. The light is pale, translucent as skim milk. Without the small berm thrown up by a snowplow an hour or so earlier it would be impossible to see the side of the road. Nothing ahead is visible, and everything closes in immediately behind. I pass through this world without a trace.

I know this road, have landmarks in my mind anchored by mileposts, the locators we use up here to know our place along this thin track. So I know there are mountains rising abruptly on my left, a declivity on my right, and more mountains lifting beyond. Driving this slowly one cannot feel any centrifugal pull on the car, and one cannot see far enough ahead to discern if the road is curving. I don't know exactly, but if I am easing around the long curve where I think I am, there is a small lake three-quarters of a mile behind the unseen trees on my left where one midnight at 35 below, under a full moon and a flittering aurora, I helped a friend pack out a moose he had killed at dusk.

Moose are not the only memory along this stretch of road. I know, too, that there are caribou around me, just over there in the trees I cannot see and moving in the invisible clearings in those invisible trees right along the road. I know they are there, though I cannot see them, for they have always been there this time of year, and they are among the earth's more dependable creatures. There will be ptarmigan also, white in their winter plumage with just a trace of brown feathers, their protective coloring a perfect match for snow and black spruce or paper birch. There will be lynx, and off somewhere in a deadfall or a cave is the cinnamon grizzly I saw last September. Twenty miles farther, the country falls off to the right, down a steep slope where I shot the last moose I will ever shoot, vowing on the spot never to do that again.

I was sitting in a little gathering at Meekins Lodge, Mile 110 on the Alcan, when a man came in and asked if anyone in our group had a moose permit and a gun. I confessed. He and his partner had seen a moose bed down near Mile 122. If I would come with them now, he said, they would show me exactly where. That year, money was not quite nonexistent but nearly so, and a moose would mean good meat at little cost.

The men were in a hurry to get to Anchorage, did not want

any more delays than necessary. There was no time to change out of my go-to-meeting oxfords, suit, and tie. My gun, a couple of knives, and a stone to sharpen them were in the car. Others in the room, rather than excusing me to do this meat-hunting chore, decided to tag along, men and women both. A small caravan of vehicles parked along the side of the road when the pickup we were following stopped. My new friend pointed out a clump of brush among the myriad clumps of brush not quite a half mile down the hill from the road and claimed the moose was "bedded down right in there."

Not really sure of my destination, I climbed the hard berm thrown up by the state plow and stepped off the back side, dropping in soft snow almost to my hips, part of me hoping there would be no moose, that he had been spooked from his nap and had moved out. The pursuit seemed absurd; having an audience for the shooting was bizarre.

Holding the .30-06 high, I floundered down the hill through the browse until the moose, rising up easily, magically, seemed to materialize before my eyes a hundred yards away. We stared at each other. It was a young bull in good shape, his rack hard and free of velvet and evenly tined. I thought, "I need you, moose, and I thank you for being here." And I also thought, "I wish you had gone away, because now I will kill you." We watched each other a moment longer. I looked back up the hill. My friends stood silently watching, a colorful row of parkaed torsos above the berm in this pale world of snow and winter light.

Given the cold, the outlandish clothes, the time it would take after the moose was down, a sensible person would have said "This is stupid" and gone back up the hill. Instead I succumbed to the scrutiny of my peers and, aware of the performance character of the event, shot the moose in the head. He collapsed directly onto himself, and I went on down to dress him out, standing beside him for a moment in my fancy duds and low shoes in the deep snow, waiting to make sure no reflexes or muscle spasms were left that might make a hoof slash out and cut my thigh or break my leg. He was so heavy I could not roll him over to begin a cut. There was no timber or snag of sufficient size to use as a lever.

Fortunately, two members of the audience were hunters and were already on their way down to help, though clothed as foolishly as I. Between us we got the moose onto his back. I draped my suit coat over a bush, rolled up my white shirtsleeves, and managed to dress out the moose, getting only minimal blood on my good slacks. I cut the carcass into chunks, knowing it would freeze before we could get back tomorrow with packs and carry it out. By the time I was finished, the afternoon was gray and cold, but even in my shirtsleeves I was sweating. We covered the carcass carefully with snow and branches from shrubs so that the ravens and magpies could not spoil the meat and climbed back up the hill, taking the heart and liver along as thanks to my friends for their help.

Even parts of a moose weigh up. The next day they had not gotten any lighter. We had cut this one into eight hefty chunks of meat. We'd lug the hide and antlers back too. The hindquarters each weighed nearly two hundred pounds. We tied one to an old wooden army pack frame and rolled it meatside down. I lay down with my back to the frame, struggled into the pack straps, rolled over onto my knees, and got up with the load. The climb to the road was steep and, dressed now for the cold, I was sweating again in a late-afternoon temperature of 25 below when I got back to the highway, gasping and with cold air rasping my throat like a bastard file, my voice a croak. I sat down right in the middle of the Alcan and disentangled myself from the pack and its frozen burden. Then I slipped and racheted back down for another load, standing off the trail we had broken so that my friends could pass, hauling themselves up as I had, grabbing handfuls of willow tops and pulling, trying not to slip or fall with their load.

I think about that moose as I drive, and of hunts for other creatures: ptarmigan, ducks, pheasants, grouse, elk, deer, rabbits,
trout, walleyes. For a time, early in my hunting days, I thought I
wanted to shoot a bear, but then I saw one close up—glistening
and graceful in her spring coat and fretful about the safety of her
cub—and the desire left me and never returned.

I can still see each one of the four moose I killed, can see
the head jerk up in a sharp pull like an intake of breath, the body
collapse straight down on itself. Once, along the south shore of
Naknek Lake, a moose came trotting toward me, apparently
oblivious of my presence. He had simply appeared from no-
where after a cold day of unsuccessful hunting on my part, ma-
terializing here before me in the open, far from any cover.
Where had he come from?

This was my last chance for meat that year, the last day of
the season, the temperature over 45 below. I was cold and tired,
and in the back of my mind, mildly apprehensive. I was alone
out there, had been dropped off that morning by Georgie Tib-
betts, a bush pilot friend. No one else knew exactly where I was.
It was getting on toward dark, 3:30 or so in the afternoon, and
Georgie was already thirty minutes overdue. If he were coming
back, hadn't had some calamity of his own, it would have to be
soon or it would be too dark for today. I got down on one knee
and let the moose come, its head swinging left and right like a
metronome. When I shot, aiming just above a line between the
eyes, its head went up and the legs folded under, as if its body
had fallen out from beneath itself. Walking the short distance to
the moose, I could hear, faint and far off but clear on the cold
air, the engine of Georgie's old Piper Tri-Pacer.

A kind of sadness lies beneath any moment of fulfillment, com-
pletion, or accomplishment. An end has been reached, yes, but
there is more, something linked to receiving a gift. One is moved
by any giving, not exactly with sadness but with a certain poig-

nant recognition that life offers grace we have not earned. There is a bond established in the anticipation of game, for hunting is a reciprocal agreement: the game gives itself to us, and we pledge to take good care of it. The bond is strengthened, a kind of love, I swear, in the sighting, which often holds an instant of consummate, tentative, fragile beauty. In the conclusion, the giving is sacramental. I do not apologize for the killing, or even regret it. To do that would demean the gift. I was grateful at the time, am grateful still for the meat and the experience and the memory of it. I was enriched and nourished by it and remain so, driving this memory of a road in the whiteout.

Hunting was an important part of my learning to find my way in the world, and for this moment in the Alcan whiteout, the road is rich with memory and speculation as I strive to find my way along it. Even traveling at five or ten miles an hour, leaning through the open window, snow stinging my face and squinting eyes, I feel I may be driving too fast. Everything is suffused with pale light as if the light were rising from a source within the earth itself. A whiteout is such a peculiar event, and this is not the first I have been in. It is the first, however, in which I was struck by the real problem whiteouts create: there is too much light, it seems to come from every direction; I am driving through a world without shadows.

Salmon push their way up the Naknek, the Kvichak, the Egegik, the Nushagak. They seem so full of their own destiny, so exact in doing exactly what they are created to do. Wolverine is perhaps the most single-minded of us all. After a fresh snow his track can be seen from a low-flying aircraft, straight as a taut cord, across a frozen lake, half a mile or more over a wooded ridge, across another lake without swerve or distraction. In a human such a track would imply destination if not destiny, an end if not a purpose. But how does wolverine know what lies ahead for him two miles or more away? Where is he going in such determined fashion? Does he know? How rare it is to find a human who can so surely find his way in the world. We are more apt to meander, struggle to determine what our destiny might be, flounder toward its fulfillment. No wonder we often feel so lost, look so longingly toward home, try so hard to make a home wherever we are. No wonder "finding ourselves" can become an obsession. In our journeying we are, at worst, traveling in a whiteout, a place with no shadows.

Without shadow, without some darkness, there is no definition to things, no shape to discern, no sense of where we are in the world, where we might go without going off the track. Darkness alone offers no guidance either. We need to have both the light and its absence at the same time. How fortunate we are, then, to have such a mixture of light and darkness within ourselves. We can be glad we are not perfect, that there are shadows we have gathered as we go. The shadows are essential to finding our way. Our awareness of the shadows in ourselves may lead us to greater tolerance of the shadows in others, may eventually lead us to that humility T. S. Eliot said is the only wisdom we can hope to acquire, perhaps the only real destiny we were born to fulfill. On this obscure trace, with ample light and inadequate vision, one understands what a poor guide the light alone is, how we need the dark.

AT THE

MERCY OF WARMTH

When I was nine or ten, I hunted squirrels with my father in the clarity of Iowa's golden October using a small, single-shot .22 rifle Pop had bought the summer before I entered fourth grade. He showed me the rifle and then put it away in his gun cabinet on the back porch. He said that I was never to take it out unless he was with me but that if I got good grades, at the end of the year it would be mine.

Northeast Iowa is on the western edge of the oak, hickory, and maple belt that once extended across the northern tier of states from Maine to the bluffs west of the Mississippi in Iowa and Minnesota. An autumn in Strawberry Point, Iowa, is as colorful as one in the maple syrup country of Vermont, the air as clear and crisp. Standing under those bright hardwoods, surrounded by some of the most domesticated landscape in America, one feels in touch with something wild and outside human control. There are squirrels in the trees, both red squirrels and gray. During the Depression we thought they were good to eat. They *were* good to eat.

When Pop had a chance, we took the .22 and went out to a hilly cow pasture beyond the edge of Dubuque. He took out the bolt, showed me the mechanism, let me hold the barrel to the sun to see its gleaming cleanliness, the twist in the rifling. He showed me how to put it all back together, how to cock the gun by pulling back on the bolt, how to hold, aim, and fire. He taught me how to take a breath and, letting it half out, squeeze the trigger so gently one could not tell when the gun would go off. I was still young enough that it was a fierce struggle to pull the bolt back to cock the rifle and harder still not to yank on the trigger when ready to fire.

The reason that first gun was a .22, Pop told me, was that it was small enough for me to handle, it had no kick, and it made for clean kills or clean misses. If you aimed badly with a .410 or twenty-gauge shotgun, the many pellets might still hurt an animal. If you shot poorly with a .22, the single bullet would most likely miss the animal entirely. Because it was a single-shot, requiring you to reload before shooting again, you had to take time to think rather than wildly firing a stream of bullets from an automatic weapon. That would be good for one's self-discipline, according to Pop, and one would have to pay more attention to his actions.

The men among my relatives, none of them far from the farm, loved to hunt. I admired those men and they hunted, so I never questioned whether hunting was a good thing to do. It was a good thing to do, and a good thing for me.

Iowa hunting in those years was mostly for pheasants, ducks, squirrels, and, occasionally in winter, cottontails. Carl and Bob Burbridge, Pop's cousins, were the storied exemplars of both speed and aim, the best wingshots anyone around there had ever known. Pop loved to tell how Carl had shot three pheasants so fast one afternoon that neither Pop nor Guy Briggs, an old hunting partner, had had time to raise their guns. I never hunted with Carl that I remember, but I never forgot the stories. I did hunt with Bob and Pop, and after a few years my brother Jack. Those times usually followed a huge Thanksgiving feast. We would eat in Marge and Dick Dopp's old farmhouse on the edge of Winthrop—a huge noon dinner of turkey and trimmings—and then go out to hunt pheasants.

Those late November days were nearly always bitter cold, often gray and snowy, and the wind would send little rivulets of hard, dry snow sifting among the broken cornstalks in the tired fields. At such times the birds would sit tight, hunkering down under a hill of cornstalks until you nearly stepped on them. Then they would flush from right beneath your feet with a great, explosive THRAAUUSSHH of wings. I would jump, startled, but Bob and Pop would simply give them a few seconds to get up and clear and then would shoot smoothly and precisely.

Learning to hunt well is largely a matter of three things. The first is learning the ways of the creatures and the cover you are going to hunt them in. The second is learning to pay attention all the time, finding the telling detail and the game in a forty-acre cornfield or on a thousand-acre canyon slope. The third is learning poise: how to control nerves strained not with anxiety but with anticipation. No matter how expectant and alert you are, the explosive sound of wings and the throaty chortle of the pheasant's voice blowing up from under your feet are an enormous surprise. There is an appropriate distance: shoot too soon and the bird will be too badly damaged by the close-packed pellets to eat; wait too long and the bird will already be out of range or the pellets will be too scattered for effect, with the bird apt to be only crippled. A certain poise is required to find that right distance, which is a space of only ten or twelve yards, in an infinite sky. For a boy, discovering that necessary adult poise in oneself, or trying to create it, is one part of the point and the wonder of hunting.

All his adult life Bob Burbridge hunted with an exuberant intensity, loved pheasant hunting more than any other kind, and his enthusiasm was infectious. Pop, too, loved it, and as a boy of eleven or twelve I loved it, relished the times we were out, and hoped that I might not disgrace myself by shooting poorly, by playing out before the men were ready to return home, or by giving in to the cold and complaining.

As the sun lowered and the temperature fell even further, we would trudge back home, kick the snow off our boots, and brush it off our pant legs with a broom. One of the men would venture a comment: "Coolin' off out there." This was not a complaint but an observation, understood to be massive understatement. Someone else would say, "A mite chilly." Then we would all troop inside and eat the cold turkey, sage dressing, and homemade bread that the women had laid out for us and finish that off with a piece of pumpkin pie topped with sweet cream whipped from the butterfat-rich, unpasteurized, unhomogenized, unseparated, unprocessed milk straight from the guernsey cow in the barn.

But that was more than a month after those clear days hunting squirrels in the October timber. That October world seemed bucolic despite our murderous purpose, incredibly peaceful and benign. Occasionally Pop and I would stop our slow walking, sit down with our backs to a tree, and watch and listen. Pop had a way of calling squirrels. The buttplate on my gun was scored with grooves just deep enough for Pop's purpose. He would take a dime from his pocket and rub its edge at varying speeds across the buttplate. The sound was remarkably like the chatter of a squirrel. I do not remember that he ever brought one in close or that they actually answered his call, but often enough one would move at the sound, scuffling through the down leaves and giving us a look as he leaped up the trunk of an adjacent tree. The intensity, focus, and clarity one tried to bring to one's vision while waiting and watching for movement was perhaps as close to prayer as I have ever come.

Though it doesn't seem wild, that autumn forest may be where I found another voice, another mind, in nature, not one all that different from my own but not always amenable to human will, just as I was not always amenable to my parents' wishes. Those squirrels and pheasants clearly had the capacity to thwart our desires. Indeed, the timbered world and its creatures had wiles with which to frustrate all reason. When not indifferent to our presence, those squirrels were out to ensure that our desire remained unfulfilled.

If it was early in the season, there would still be many leaves on the trees, making squirrels hard to see even when you could hear them or see the leaves and tiny branches shake with their passing. Squirrels were adept at making use of such cover, hiding themselves, freezing in place behind a clump of leaves and outwaiting a hunter. If it was late in the fall and the leaves had dropped, the squirrels were exposed. Then, if they heard you coming, they would slide around the trunk and keep it between you and their bodies. You could circle the tree and the squirrel would circle too, never showing itself, sixty feet or more in the tree, or showing itself so briefly that there was no time to draw a bead. When I was old enough to hunt on my own, I often went into the timber by myself. I would circle trees fruitlessly, occasionally reaching down for a stick or a rock I could toss past the tree to rustle the leaves on the far side, trying to dupe the squirrel into thinking someone was over there so he would move to my side of the trunk. Fewer than one in a hundred would fall for such a shameless ruse, though it always remained in my bag of tricks, a bag kept small by my lack of imagination.

Perhaps such creatures lack the capacity for thought, but then I must share the lack as well, for they persistently outwitted me. Some insist that such actions are mere instinct, not the product of thought. But then one thinks of the determination with which squirrels gather food for storage. That too may be the result of instinct, not thought, but I did not care how others explained it. For me there was a mind at work in nature as a whole that was too complicated for dismissal, too perfect in its workings to be random or accidental, too exciting and compelling to be overlooked.

At times during those fall days I would become totally immersed in that natural mind, not exactly awestruck but swept up, anchored and yet adrift, exultant and lost in something so huge it was at once mysterious, incomprehensible, thrilling, beautiful, exalted, still, peaceful, tumultuous, haunting, momentous, and timeless, both benign and dangerous. If those words do not all fit together, if some seem contradictory, then I am describing accurately what I felt. How is it that one can feel and see with such absolute clarity yet find the feeling so confusing? Perhaps what I felt is what some American Indians would call the Power. There was power out there, and I was surrounded by it, immersed in it, part of it and yet aware of something like otherness.

All this, of course, is hindsight. At nine or fourteen all I knew was that there were times I felt I might burst or levitate, that the clear air and bright hardwood colors could not contain either the stillness or the tumult that was inside me. For nearly twenty-five years that exaltation was to come most often when I was hunting.

After I moved to Montana I learned to hunt medium-sized game such as deer and antelope from Bob DeVries of Roberts and got to hunt elk for the first time through the courtesy of Joe Reese of Ft. Lauderdale, Florida. I had spent the previous four years in Boston and Reading, Massachusetts, attending Boston University's School of Theology. In that time I had not picked up a gun. After I moved to Montana, Bob invited me out to his dry-land ranch outside Roberts one bright autumn Saturday. He and a couple of friends were going to sight-in their rifles in preparation for the opening of antelope season. Although I could not as yet claim residency and a resident's hunting license, I was naturally curious and interested.

Jim Croft set the lid from a coffee can in the side of a dirt bank a hundred yards from Bob's house, then sat down and wrapped his arm through the sling of his rifle for a firm anchor. It had been an afternoon of mutual joshing, and though greenhorn and ignorant, I joined in the teasing. Just before Jim squeezed off his shot, I said, "If you can't hit that offhand, you should give it all up." Jim looked up, surprised. "If you can hit it offhand, I'll give you my antelope permit," he challenged. Though I had never fired a high-powered rifle before, it could not be any different in principle from firing a .22, I thought, so I took him up on it. When the .270 went off, I was so astonished at the sound and the kick that I did not see the lid fall from its perch in the dirt, but I heard the men laughing and knew I had scored before I saw it.

Jim issued additional challenges immediately. We switched to an old Winchester .22 pump that was a favorite of Bob's. Jim threw up a chunk of dirt from the field and yelled. I pulled up and hit it. He threw other clods into the air and I hit them all. I had never been able to do that before in my life. I was as astonished as anyone at what was happening and far more puzzled, though I tried to maintain an air that suggested custom. I did not think it necessary to tell them that I had never possessed, let alone exhibited, such skill before. Neither did I report later that I was never able to do it again. I had learned the virtues of such silences from reading about Joe Meek, a mountain man who once charged a war party of Blackfeet single-handedly and turned apparent defeat into a rout of the enemy. He accepted the congratulations of his companions but said later, "I did not deem it necessary to tell them that I could not hold my horse."

The first time Bob DeVries and I hunted deer together in Montana we piled into his pickup to head for the shallow canyon carved through the dry hills by Rock Creek. At the bottom of a ravine where he thought there might be deer, there were deer—five of them, including two bucks. They spooked before we got off a good shot, running up the draw and out of sight. "I know where they're going," said Bob, and we headed back to his pickup. When we got back to the top of the draw, we could see the deer, already far off, trotting stiff-legged through a long field of summer fallow now covered by snow. Bob turned in another direction, drove a few miles cross-country, turned again, drove a few miles farther, and stopped by a snow-covered stubble field. "They'll be over here in a little coulee," Bob said as we got out.

We walked quickly up a long, low slant of ridge and across a flat stretch, stumbling occasionally and breaking through the crusty snow.

A little over half a mile out, Bob stopped. There is a break a little way ahead, he told me, and the deer will be holed up in it. We should be very quiet but can walk almost to the edge before they will see us. "Hunker down a bit," he warned. "The wind is right. If those two bucks are here, they'll run when we get to the top of the draw. You take the one on the left, I'll take the right." I could not see any break in the landscape, really didn't have a clue as to what Bob was talking about, but we walked a few rods and suddenly a steep little coulee opened up beneath us. Five deer leaped up and ran. We each got a buck.

Joe Reese and his wife, Hattie, were traveling through Red Lodge and had come to church on Sunday morning. This was when I was the pastor of the little three-point Methodist parish that included Red Lodge, Roberts, and Luther. Joe allowed that he and Hattie were up from Florida, just traveling around, getting in a little fishing and planning to go elk hunting later in the fall. They were camped out on the edge of town and thought they might hang around a few days, the country was so pretty.

That fall Joe signed on to hunt elk up behind Cook City with a local guide and rodeo hand named Bill Dygart. Joe asked if I would come along. He'd checked it out with Bill and the arrangements were all taken care of. I couldn't get away for the whole time, but I went for a few days. Those September days in the high country pussyfooting for elk seemed just like the October days I had spent hunting squirrels in Iowa. The vegetation was different, but the air had that clear, cold tang to it, and the method was the same. I was surprised at the correspondences and I thought, "I know how to do this."

There were some differences too. We had been climbing over some steep caprock, which required the horses to put their feet precisely in particular crannies or else there would be no purchase. I saw my mare's right front hoof miss the spot and began to shuck the stirrups as she began to slide backward, scrabbling to stay upright. Bill and Joe, who had gone ahead, turned at the clatter and yelled, "Get off, Gary, get off!" I was thinking, "I am, dammit, I am!" but was too busy to yell. When I did shake loose and bail out to the left, the little mare began to right herself. She got her footing at the bottom of the rock and so did I. The second time up, with the mare trembling—though no more than I was—we had no difficulty.

I didn't get an elk that trip, didn't even see one, though we heard one bugle across a deep canyon close to dark, and for me the eerie echo of it remains one of the greatest sounds in all nature. I left camp then, following a supplier's pack-string back down over the caprock and through the black spruce, happy to have been out in those mountains, happy to be heading back on horseback, while Joe stayed in camp another week and got the elk he wanted.

How does one move from hunting passionately to drifting away from it? It may have begun with the deer I saw at dawn, perhaps the most beautiful sight I ever saw in the mountains. Or with the moose resting in a clump of brush in Alaska. But the real beginning lay in a choice that I did not know had anything to do with deer or moose.

I was young, still restless, and I asked my wife for a divorce. We had two children. She was shocked and hurt. Casual friends were astonished and dismayed; the Montana church congregations were stunned; our best friends, discovering I was serious, were angry. I had just sense enough to recognize that their anger came from disappointment and to know that, painful as it might be, they were worth my taking some lumps so we could survive this and remain friends. We talked it all around, if not out, none of us conceding much.

At the time I recognized that what I was doing was certainly the most selfish thing I had ever done, perhaps the most selfish thing I would ever do. Oh, I had a long list of grievances in my head. They seemed serious then, but in a few years I couldn't remember just what they were. I was not behaving at my best by a long shot. I hardly got the words to my wife out of my mouth than I started seeing someone else, became evasive and occasionally deceitful and self-protective. I did not fall from grace but leaped headlong.

Some aspects of the decision were liberating. Many folks in any congregation assume that their pastor is "good." When one knows himself to be otherwise, knows that there is a darker aspect to his life, regardless of profession, that can become a heavy burden, eventually an intolerable one, and a sense of hypocrisy grows inside. When folks discovered that I was leaving, they were shocked, but I couldn't help feeling something like, "Well, at least now you know," and that was a real lifting of the burden, an important and appropriate shift from the earlier, "If you only knew . . ."

There were also more painful complications to the decision. My parents were more unhappy than I had feared, and I had feared enough. They could not understand my feelings or buy my clumsy explanations at all. The morning after I told them, at their home in Kansas City, that I wanted to get a divorce, Mom came upstairs to tell me I'd better leave, just get out of the house. "No, don't call," she said. "Your dad is too upset. Maybe in time we'll call you, but you should be gone before he comes up." I left.

The folks weren't the only ones. No one I knew thought I might be doing the right thing. Everyone insisted that I should do the hard thing and go back. What no one could understand was that there was so much pressure to do that, so many demands to do that, that it would have been the easy thing to do. It would have brought me back—at least partway—from disgrace into the fold of friendship. Life could regain something, perhaps, of its former shape and contours. But I didn't really believe that. I had bent things so far out of shape that they could never recover their former contours. What I also knew, and could not admit to others, was that going back would put me in greater jeopardy than staying away. I knew that if I went back I would do something even more foolish and desperate. What I expected, mostly earned and received, was rejection and rebuff from nearly every friend I had.

I left Red Lodge, Roberts, and Luther, and the ministry—a shift in profession almost as difficult and painful as the rift in my personal relations. I had cherished those three small communities and had relished a clergyman's freedom. I had discovered that those parishioners were ministering more to me than I ever could to them and were more appreciative of my fumbling and ineptness than I had any right to expect. Despite modest accomplishments, I had learned some things about that work and had even won some rare praise. One example of that came from an old rancher who was drunk one night and introduced me to a friend: "I want you to meet the best god-damned preacher . . ." There were other examples, however, that were more telling.

One day of hard snow and high wind when Joe was gone, his wife's father died. I had a day off and was doing some woodworking when the undertaker called. I became pretty grumpy. I did not want to go out to the ranch; it was miles off the county road, and the lane down the coulee to the house was apt to be drifting badly. I could see myself getting stuck. Neither Joe nor his wife, Irene, had any connection with the church. Further, Irene and I had met once before, when she was in the hospital, and it had not been a particularly pleasant visit. She seemed angry, in part because I did not seem able to pronounce her name right. How can you mispronounce Papez? After she had corrected me a couple of times, it was clear she did not know the answer to that question, and I felt pretty stupid. There was also a sense growing in me (one that had nothing to do with either Irene or Joe) that the conventional religious comforts all fall

short, that there was nothing I could say that would make everything all right. I was struggling with the idea that I had gone
into this work for the wrong reasons. Now I was not anxious to
face Irene again.

Nevertheless, I stowed my gear, jumped into the car, and set
out. As I'd expected, the ranch lane was drifting badly. Halfway
into the ranch and with snow flying up over my front bumper,
the thought came to me: "What are you complaining about,
Holthaus? This is exactly what you were born to do." I laughed
out loud, all alone out there in the flying snow. Even though I
had nothing to say that would make things all right, I pulled up
outside the ranch house happy to be there. "Mrs. Papez, Tom
told me about your father."

Inside, I sat on a couch in the tiny living room while Irene
made tea. I thought the lamp on my end of the couch was sitting on an end table, but when I looked a second time I discovered that it was really resting on stacks of paperback books, a
great pile of them, six or eight books square, stacked neatly and
nearly two feet high. At the other end of the couch was another
such table. They were all westerns. I asked if Joe read all these
westerns. Irene said no, she did. Since I'd read nearly all of them
too, we talked about the books. We also talked about her father,
Irene reminiscing about events both funny and sad. We made
some arrangements for an obituary and the funeral and had a
fine visit. I left on a cloud, driving easily, snow flying, back out
the lane without getting stuck.

At home again, I was sanding boards at about eight o'clock
in the evening when there was a knock at the door. Joe stood
there covered with snow. He wouldn't come into the house, he
said, wouldn't take my time.

"I just came 'cause I wanted to thank you," he said, "for going out to see the missus this afternoon. I got home just an hour
or so after you left, and she was so happy you'd come. Said she
couldn't believe anybody'd go clear out to our place just to
see her, and in the snow an' all. She was feeling so good, I just
wanted to let you know that I really appreciate it." He turned

back to his pickup and drove off in the snow falling in the street-light's yellow glow.

In those days a divorce was much less common than it has become over the past thirty-five years, and for a clergyman the whole context of such an event was far more strained than it is now. The church did not handle it much better than I did. The bishop explained to me, kindly, that I was out, that the church ought to stand for something better than I represented. I couldn't deny that. He did not take my credentials away, but he would not have me serve a congregation either. My life shifted from one in which I was appreciated too much to one in which I was scorned or disdained.

I lived for a year in the basement of a house that belonged to some friends in Dillon. They had a kind of student hostel, and I had a bunk bed in a room with a couple of summer school students. Summer school offered me a start so that I could get certified to teach. To those who knew me but not well, I must have seemed to be off on a new, selfish, and destructive adventure. In truth I was broke, tired, scared, cowed by the loss of friends, and, knowing the pain I was causing others, weakened by my sense of a diminished self. To the church I had become a kind of moral toxic waste. A preacher from Billings wrote to tell my host that he ought not to let me stay in his basement, for it did not reflect well on his moral judgment and I would certainly be a bad influence on any college kids who stayed there.

That summer Ben and Phyl Karas came to Dillon from Red Lodge to fish the Beaverhead and the Big Hole. They were still a bit puzzled and sad but accepting. They had run into the county sheriff, with whom I had often hunted and fished, and they brought a letter from him, the only other kind word I heard that summer. He wrote that he didn't want to make any judgments because he knew that when people went home after work at five o'clock and closed the door, no one knew what went on. He signed it, "Your friend, Jim." It would be months before there were a couple of other reconciliations and reconnections.

Later that fall the sheriff, Jim Eichler, called to tell me that he and a couple of friends were taking horses to go elk hunting up on the Line Creek Plateau behind Mount Maurice. He wanted me to come along. I was wary, wondering about the others. He assured me that everyone wanted me to come and that Ben would be there. I went, hungry not for the hunting but for the companionship of those men. We had three days of tough hunting, cold weather, and little game. Jim got a deer while he and Ben and I were sitting on a high rim, dangling our feet over the ledge and looking for elk across the canyon. I looked straight down just as a big buck walked out on a rocky ledge directly below. "Look at that," I whispered, pointing down. Jim swept his gun around, pointed it down between his knees and shot the deer. Realizing the hard and perhaps dangerous work he had created for us, he let a contrite expression and an impish grin fight for control of his face. "Temporary insanity," he said. We managed to climb down the rocky wall of the canyon, dress out the deer on the narrow ledge, and horse the carcass, heart, and liver back up to the rim where we'd been sitting. When Jim wanted to go back for the horns, we laughed and watched him. It turned out that that one deer was our only meat to show for the trip.

On the way back down after the hunt, standing cold and stiff in the saddle, legs straight to ease the weight on the horse, I saw a big deer standing frozen above us in the timber, watching our procession. I automatically hauled the .30-06 from its scabbard and bailed off the horse, feet so cold that they stobbed into the ground like tent pegs. Jim was behind me and did the same. I laid the rifle across the saddle and looked through the scope. I knew I could kill the deer. It was an easy head shot; the deer would feel nothing. In my mind I shot it, saw it tumble down toward us, an easy kill, easy to pack out. I could do it, but I did not *want* to do it.

That buck was beautiful, and he represented a kind of beauty I wanted, needed, in the world. Beauty had become combined in my mind with an absence of pain, and the absence of pain with a sense of life's equally touching and fragile sweetness. Goodness, truth, and beauty had become inseparable in my mind that fall. The world was too full of hurt, too sorely in need of beauty, my own life too much in need of truth and goodness. For me there was a direct tie: To take away or diminish beauty was to increase pain. I had come to see everyone I knew (and assumed it to be true of those I didn't) as making their way through the world like the walking wounded. I was still so tender in my own mind that the idea of adding to the world's pain was not tolerable. Later, of course, there would be other times, many other times, when my choices would cause pain in others, but for this moment, even if this death would be painless, it meant an end to a very certain beauty, and beauty of any kind had become essential.

The others along the trail behind me were growing impatient. "Shoot," Ben whispered. I kept watching the deer through the scope but didn't pull the trigger. Jim finally pulled a gun and took the shot as the deer began to move. He missed. I was glad. I remounted, stiff and cold and unable to explain what had happened as we continued down the trail in our separate silences to the car and the long drive back to Dillon.

I had steeled myself to fend off the onslaught of a society that was simply trying to protect itself from the kind of disintegration my actions represented. My feelings were so close to the surface that I had learned to anticipate emotional dangers so that nothing could catch me off-guard or crack the shell of poise I had erected, a further refinement of that discipline one develops as a kid out hunting.

That fall I had begun teaching at the junior high in Dillon. The paychecks helped, but they were small and the need for money was pressing. I sold off all my old camping gear and hunting equipment. Years before, I had acquired an old Colt navy revolver in a trade. I knew that Vern Waples, the game warden in Red Lodge, might want to buy it and that he would not take advantage of me. I called and asked if he was interested, and he allowed as how he might be. One night after school I drove over to Red Lodge, made my way to Vern's, and knocked on his door in the dark. I had not seen him since I'd left town and had no idea how he might feel toward me. I admired him greatly but knew that his own code was often unyielding, as befits a lawman. I prepared myself to face him. The door opened and the yellow light came blinding, leaving Vern in silhouette. "Well," he said, "the world's been kinda tough on you lately." I wasn't sure I'd heard him correctly.

It is possible to be so far down that one can brace oneself for any negative response, any potential rebuke, make oneself impervious, though not indifferent, to any rejection. After a time nothing from that side of our social discourse, no matter how harsh, can crack one's poise. One may even begin to take strength from it, toughen oneself for whatever comes. What I had not expected, had not thought to prepare for or steel myself against, was warmth. Vern's words were such a change from what I had been hearing—that it was I who was being tough on the world— that it blindsided me. I stayed on the porch in the shadows, swallowing fast, mumbled something about how pretty it was out there under the stars, undone by his unexpected warmth. Years later the phrase "at the mercy of warmth" would occur in a poem about Smitty, my Alaska friend who had died of cancer. The metaphor that came was of ice on the Yukon River breaking up in spring, at the mercy of the sun. But I was aware that the origin of the phrase, and the thought behind it, was from a different scene with a different meaning, a word from years before, so unexpected in its gentleness that I was unstrung.

AT THE
HEART OF THE HEART
OF THE UNIVERSE

There is only one question:
How to love this world.

—Mary Oliver

To be truly free one must take on the basic conditions
as they are—painful, impermanent, open, imperfect—
and then be grateful for impermanence and the
freedom it grants us. For in a fixed universe there
would be no freedom.

—Gary Snyder

I was at a personal milestone: my fiftieth birthday. It seemed
a good time to get away from everything for a spell, take stock of
my life in a spare desert setting that would force it. With life
pared down to a backpack and my own personal resources, I
would see if certain outdoor skills that might have atrophied after years of city living were indeed lost. If so, perhaps the land itself would help me regain them.

I wanted to be in country where I'd had some special experiences before, and I was eager to have some time to myself after
several hectic months of work and travel. Part of my purpose
was to check out the lay of a land that was to appear in *Circling
Back,* a book I'd been working on. I was mindful, too, that the
exertion involved would not be all that different from the effort

put forth by Bashō, the great Japanese poet, who took his journey into the interior, into the far north of Japan, for some of the same reasons I had and at the same age.

I walked from south central Montana down into central Wyoming, a couple of hundred miles from Red Lodge to Shoshone, staying away from marked trails and highways as much as possible and trying to see the terrain the way a person might have in the nineteenth century traveling cross-country to rendezvous with friends. Along the way I soon found myself once again living in the midst of nature's indifference.

My route began a few miles above Red Lodge, where I crossed Rock Creek on an irrigation headgate and then climbed the first alluvial ridges spilling off the flanks of Mount Maurice. One can still see the travois ruts left there by Crows in the nineteenth century. They loved this part of the country, and some wintered on the mild slopes of this southeastern end of the Beartooth Mountains.

I moseyed along the lower edge of the timber and then climbed up into the mixed conifers where steep little coulees and gullies made for hard walking. Following a deer trail, I actually came upon deer: four muleys, as surprised to run into me as I was to find them. Coming back down along the old stagecoach road that once ran from Red Lodge to Meeteetse, Wyoming, I spooked a coyote that sprang over the ridge and disappeared. I stopped to look over the country from a jumble of rocks on a sagebrush ridge above Bearcreek. From there I could see the valley of the Clarks Fork of the Yellowstone and beyond its pale riparian green the Pryor Mountains and farther south to the Bighorns. I could see three whitetails too, moving cautiously below me, and then, hot but feeling good, I had a drink, climbed down, and moved on. A jackrabbit came loping directly toward me until just a few feet away and then, startled, he put on the brakes and suddenly veered, zig-zagging off downcountry in long leaps.

On the South Fork of Grove Creek, I boiled a couple of pots of water and put them into the creek to cool while I took note of the grotto. The ford where the Meeteetse stage used to cross the creek lies in a small clearing with cottonwoods and firs along the edges, all nestling in a deep little gulch between two sagebrush ridges. Palisades of Madison limestone tower above a sharp cleft in the rock where the South Fork comes through. The old stage route continues up a grade so steep that passengers had to walk to the top or the horses could not pull the stage. The trails left by both the stages and the passengers were still clearly visible after ninety-five years.

I poured the cool water from the billies into canteens and boiled more water for coffee. While I sipped the coffee, storms dropped thin veils of rain on the Clarks Fork to the south and east. There were clouds in the mountains too. This was a good place to be if it rained, the big cottonwoods making it easy to rig a tarp and stay dry, and the trees providing plenty of fuel. There would be another three hours of daylight, and the next water was about eight miles away as the crow flies. I'd assumed I'd camp here, for I expected to be tired by the time I got this far. Instead it was early, and though I had sweated buckets getting here, I felt fine. Restless, I went on.

I left the South Fork with the two quarts of water I'd boiled. A couple of hours later I was too far from the creek to go back but far enough from the next water that the following day could be difficult. The terrain was more up and down than I had expected, and my feet were growing sore. At dusk I hit a great pile of rimrock and a rock face that I couldn't climb at the head of Mill Creek Draw, so I stumbled down to camp in a tiny cottonwood grove, disturbing a deer but not, apparently, the red ants that gathered around me in great numbers until the cold drove them underground. I built a fire, made some biscuits using foil for a reflector, and rolled into my sleeping bag dead tired.

Dawn came on hot, and the temperature quickly rose to well over ninety degrees. I made coffee and Cream o' Wheat for breakfast, leaving me with just a pint of water to get me to Line Creek. I was tired and sore, and I discovered that though the land looks easy, it is an endless succession of low ridges with steep, rocky sides, coulees, and rimrock—hard going, totally absent of shade or water. The wind came on hard and I tied my straw hat down with a thong.

At ten in the morning I shrugged out of my pack and set it down against some sagebrush. The cool green of the pack instantly became the tallest thing around for shade. Already fairly played out, I finished what little water I had and looked off at Line Creek about seven miles away. I could not see the creek but could see the willows along it, stringing down from the mountains and tailing off into the desert where the creek would be. I thought, "I don't know whether I can walk that far without water or not," and remembered that aside from occasionally hunting pheasants or ducks or fishing for trout along the Clarks Fork, I knew this country mostly from looking down at it from the top of the Line Creek Plateau, where water was always easy to come by. Instead of being a veteran in this high-plains desert, I was a rube and would prove it more than once.

I started again and tried to choke down a granola bar without water. The heat had begun to be a serious drain. It was so hot, as the old sheriff used to say, that even the flies were walking. Late in the afternoon I arrived at the creek and stood by the bank, knowing I shouldn't drink without boiling the water first. For a long time I studied a place that had been fenced off so that calves could cross at a ford in the stream. I was trying to sort out whether I wanted to be on the upstream or the downstream side of the crossing to avoid the contamination stirred up by the calves. I started a fire, stooped over to fill my billy, and fell into the water face first.

A few days later I walked into Cody, Wyoming, and splurged on a room in the old wing of the Irma Hotel. I patched up my feet, drank buckets of water, and spent the first hours in my room staring vacantly, mind-numbed, at the wall—not reading, not thinking, just staring. Next day I went looking for maps. I love the USGS topographic maps but had discovered that some of them had not been updated since 1954. During the interval, land reclamation and irrigation had lowered the water table in this region so far that many of the beautiful little blue lines that spelled water were in reality dry washes that should have been brown.

That weekend Ben Karas, a longtime partner of mine in outdoor ventures, came over to fish with me on the South Fork of the Shoshone. I told him about running short of water and laughed at my puzzlement over whether to stop up- or downstream from the cattle crossing. Ben, a fine medical doctor, just shook his head at my story. Given the heat and the wind out there, he told me, you can lose a liter of liquid an hour, and my two-quart-a-day supply was inadequate. The symptoms for dehydration, he added, are pretty much the same as those for hypothermia: the first thing to go is your brains, "not that you've got that many," and you make dangerous choices without realizing it. Next day I bought two more bottles for water.

What we want most, perhaps, is to have another person acknowledge that our life is acceptable as it is, not for what it might become or what it ought to be but is not. Such acceptance is one definition of freedom. It is also one definition of wholeness, for we do not have to excise any part of our life or expurgate the story of it that we tell ourselves or the world. Love sometimes begins by offering this. If, after the flash of attraction, after time together, after the sexual desire has been explored, there is not this acknowledgement, then things may come apart.

What poets Gary Snyder and Mary Oliver both seem to want most is to live with a clear-eyed vision of the nature of this world and to accept everything in their purview with gratitude, in Snyder's case, or love, in Oliver's. For both of them, love and freedom come from "the basic conditions as they are." Those conditions, Snyder admits, are "painful, impermanent, open, imperfect." Our necessity, then, is to learn gratitude, to "be grateful for impermanence and the freedom it grants us." In this he speaks directly from his Buddhist tradition and echoes many indigenous people around the world.

"There is only one question," Mary Oliver holds. "How to love this world." The context is a vivid description of a spring bear coming down the mountain for her. Both poets claim that learning to look nature in the eye and accept it as it is—pain, impermanence, and all—is a way, perhaps the only way, to love the world, to live with the gratitude that not only establishes our freedom but also lends coherence to our understanding of the world. It might also be the way to live in the world without generating fear in the animals we call wild.

If we look at the world with that poised and undaunted eye, what do we see at the heart of the universe? Rilke, the German poet, was once taken, at his own request, out into the Swiss countryside and left to himself for the day. In a short time he was frantic to get back to civilization. He could not tolerate the abyss of indifference he felt at the heart of nature. It was an unbearable burden.

Most of us who have been alone for a time in a wild setting have felt this. Apparently Rilke was shocked and overwhelmed by it. On a ridge five or ten miles from the nearest road, surrounded by sagebrush and a vista that reveals nothing human, anxious for water and not knowing any nearby sources, the apparent indifference of this desert land is powerful. It is clear that nothing out there in that high-plains sagebrush desert cares whether you live or die.

Yet indifference seems the key to something important in wild nature, whether that be sagebrush desert, mountain fastness, or urban jungle. In the desert I was facing, such a dry world is not a hostile world. Wild nature is no more bent on harm than it is on help. It has no intent of any kind toward us; it is simply present. Out there, standing under an eagle circling high, one feels the wheeling of the galaxy, aware of the movement, large and small, of everything swirling around. It is easy in such a place to feel we are at the center of the universe. This is not to say that we have a position of importance. The old Greeks are criticized these days for putting man at the center of the universe, but in their view that was not a position of superiority, as we assume. Aristotle believed that the center was like a sump. All the world's detritus swirled down into it. Rather than being a cause for pride, being at the center made man the equivalent of the rest of the world's garbage.

Perhaps that center we imagine in the wilderness feels like indifference because it is balanced at the exact center between the malign and the benign. These are not opposites; rather, they both dance at the circumference of the world, are strung all along every radius, equidistant from T. S. Eliot's "still point at the center of the turning world." No wonder the purpose of so many indigenous peoples is to maintain balance, to live with such respect that if the weight should shift, it will be back toward the center, toward the benign. Nature will not do anything either to take your life or prolong it. It will be whatever it is, neither more nor less, a permanent mix of wolves and doves.

Standing one morning on the central Wyoming desert just west of Rhyolite, an eagle circling overhead, mountains rising behind, the great high desert stretching out downcountry, I was struck not only by the vast indifference of nature but also by a sudden sense of well-being, as if it were all right to be where I was, even to be what I was. What I felt was far beyond desert, eagle, mountains, and sky—beyond the land itself. It came from behind that larger nature that encompasses earth's natural systems, behind the great facade of indifference. Rilke didn't look hard enough. Yes, there is indifference at the heart of this entirely natural world. But caught up within that indifference we all sense at the heart of the heart of the universe there also lies a kind of acceptance, and there is freedom in that acceptance.

That profound indifference in the world beyond our doorstep is liberating, for it exerts no pressure to conform to the expectations of others. There is nothing out there that wishes you were anything other than what you are. At the pulsing heart of the heart of the universe beats an acceptance of one's whole nature, both the wolf and the dove inside one's soul. Though nature seems to exhibit no feeling toward us at all, it finally offers us the freedom to be whatever we are without excuse or cover, one of the deepest names we have for love. Nature's indifference is the source, the fountainhead, of an etiquette of freedom that Snyder says we can learn from the wild. That acceptance is also one source of the solace that the wilderness offers us. How can we respond except to take on the world, the whole of its conditions, with gratitude, to learn to love even "the dazzling blackness" coming down to consume us. Acceptance becomes mutual. The world accepts us; we accept the world.

Nearly always our presence in the field implies a threat. I approach antelope, they run away; I get close to a magpie, it flies. Once I saw a golden eagle circling and walked over toward the ridge above which she was hunting. She veered off. After hiking on down to Meeteetse and Thermopolis through the Wind River Canyon, the Bighorn River sliding by in some stretches without a sound, I had come close enough to animals and birds that I began to wonder how to be among them without generating the fear that drives them away. How could I approach without having other creatures flee? That eagle had drifted to another ridge, then dropped, settling on a rocky outcrop. That rock held nothing of fear for an eagle.

I camped for several days at Boysen Reservoir and made day hikes out from there. One afternoon a band of antelope, curious as ever, circled me slowly, working their way closer. After a time they came down from a ridge, crossed a coulee, and moved right up the ridge I was on. They stopped, staring at me, and two stepped closer as if they were a delegation. They barked several times while I remained partially concealed, waving my hat in the same consistent motion I'd been making since I first observed them. Their sound was a mix of bleat, bark, and cough. I had never heard them do this when I had hunted them years before. Feeling foolish and glad no one was around, I barked a tentative bark back. They looked at me, barked, took a few mincing steps closer, stopped, bleated again, and advanced a bit more. I simply stood there. When I finally moved, they beat a moderately hasty retreat with no further barking and no alarms other than the raised white hair on their rumps, and flight. With one stop to look back, they disappeared over a ridge.

Later, talking about this with my son, Kevin, an experienced outdoorsman, he asked if it seemed that the antelope were asking for some identification. That was exactly right. "Let us know who you are," they were barking. It was possible that if I had had a proper ID, I might have had a different relationship to the creatures out there.

It seemed clear that I could not establish a relationship that did not engender fear until I had settled some prior questions: How do I find my proper place here? How can I fit in so that I exhibit the acceptance that seems immanent in the heart of nature and that overcomes fear—not my fear but the fear I engender in others? How do I, or any of us, live so that the permission to exist that wild nature gives us extends through us to other creatures?

It seemed possible that the model could be a tree or a rock, so indifferent as to cause no harm, generate no fear. At the base of the limestone outcrop a cottontail squats in the shade, a snake curls on the ledge, a magpie clings to the snag that extends from a fissure. Nothing is afraid of rock. Nothing is afraid to settle in, on, or near a tree. Bird and insect, eagle and sparrow, owl and crow all settle fearlessly in its branches. Harder to discern is the fact that in simply being, both rock and tree open themselves, give themselves to the world. The rock opens itself to water, surrenders to a wedge of ice, gives wind some grit, makes room for dirt and roots and resting creatures, gives itself infinitesimal bit by bit to the world. Nothing fears or feels compelled to flee either the rock or the tree, which simply are. They neither bluster nor threaten nor pose. They wear no civilized mask.

If I could learn to look at nature straight on, accepting its basic conditions, I might find myself the beneficiary of a giant reciprocity, might be at ease in the heart of courtesy as one participant in a nature that offers acceptance, and therefore the freedom to be, behind its apparently blind indifference. If I could purge myself of all intent toward animals, including the intent to avoid frightening them (for that desire includes a demand: Don't be afraid), if I could become indifferent as rock or tree, without a claim of any kind on other creatures, they might not flee. My identity, then, would become "creature indifferent to us, not bent on harm."

Just discovering the notion of indifference may be enough to change one's attitude. One morning I set out along a line fence, and a magpie, as if waiting for me, let me approach within fifteen feet, apparently unafraid. Then it flew down the fence a ways and waited again until I caught up and passed it within a yard or so and then flew on ahead and waited again. We went down the line like this for perhaps half a mile.

But I wondered how antelope might react. I confess that I am a bit of a freak about antelope. Off and on for several years I wore a little pot-metal medallion with the embossed figure of an antelope on it. If I were entitled to a totem animal, and entitled to choose among them, I would choose antelope. In all this dry country, they are, except for a few sluggish streams, the most fluid thing around. Their smooth run is so different from a deer's bound. The antelope's rocking canter smoothes out in a hard run like a greyhound's. They seem so effortless in this that they rarely appear to be moving as fast as they actually are, flowing with barely a ripple over the sagebrush. For forty million years their line has been moving over these prairies like the stroke of a calligrapher's brush.

I admire antelope less for their famous speed than for two other characteristics: the acuity of their great vision, which combines a long-range view of the world with an eye for the telling detail; and their intense curiosity, which sometimes lures them into trouble. They are the great observers and examiners of all in their domain. We rightly admire the eyes of the hawk, but antelope can discern a moving object eight miles off and a small stationary object more than a mile away. While several rest on a sidehill, one or two will stand watch, their eyes taking in anything that might represent danger. Further, they are prone to investigate, curiosity leading them closer and closer to anything that seems inexplicable or beyond experience even if the investigation leads them into danger. Old-time hunters had only to tie a rag on some sagebrush and sooner or later antelope would come circling closer and closer to discern exactly what this mysterious fluttering was. In time they would circle close enough to be in range for a shot.

One reason to keep antelope and other wild creatures around us is that they have these two characteristics worthy of emulation: the great vision to capture all the world before one, and the curiosity to keep on investigating that world until it is impossible to look closer and think harder, until death finally brings an end to the search forever. If antelope were humans, they would be what we used to call natural philosophers.

Perhaps cultivating indifference is not the real clue to reducing fear in other creatures. Maybe all we need to learn is to forget everything we think we know and simply be present to the world. On another day, mind empty of everything but what I could see before me, I topped a little ridge and surprised a lone antelope dozing near a pond. He jumped up, looked me over, then visibly relaxed. He barked. I barked back. He took a few hesitant steps toward me, and I continued on my course, oblique to his. He came closer, then walked alongside, grazing, occasionally lagging but then cantering up, never more than fifteen yards away, for over a mile. When we came upon a doe, he wandered over to her and they ambled off together.

Reassured by our indifference, antelope or other creatures may come calling, asking who we are, ready to visit. Then, for at least one luminous, irrefutable moment, we will know our place in the world and will find it home at last.

ABOUT THE AUTHOR

Gary Holthaus grew up in Iowa and has lived in New England, Montana, Alaska, and Colorado. He received a bachelor's degree from Cornell College in Mount Vernon, Iowa; bachelor and master of sacred theology degrees from Boston University; and a master of science in education degree from Western Montana College.

Holthaus is the author of *Unexpected Manna,* a collection of poems from Copper Canyon Press; *Circling Back,* a poetic treatment of the history of the American West; and *Traveling Alone: Eight Days in Autumn,* a chapbook about travels in several western states. With Robert Hedin he edited *Alaska: Reflections on Land and Spirit* and *The Great Land: Reflections on Alaska,* both published by the University of Arizona Press. His other nonfiction works include *Teaching Eskimo Culture to Eskimo Students, Handbook for Bilingual Education,* which he edited, and *Alaska Native Orators, Storytellers, and Writers,* which he edited with Richard and Nora Dauenhauer. Among other awards, Holthaus has received an Individual Artist's Fellowship in Poetry from the National Endowment for the Arts, was selected as Outstanding Alaska Humanist for 1991, and was cited in "Notable American Essays, 1994," by Robert Atwan, general editor of the Best American Essays series.

Holthaus currently resides in Red Wing, Minnesota, where he is the executive director of the Anderson Center for Inter-disciplinary Studies. Holthaus's son and daughter, Kevin and Stephanie, both grew up in the West and live in Alaska. His wife, Lauren Pelon, is a musician who has performed in many parts of the world.